Editor
Tom Finley

Consulting Editors
Marian Wiggins
Annette Parrish
Carol Eide

Contributing Writer
Sandy Larsen

Designed and Illustrated by Tom Finley

The standard Bible text used in this course is the Holy Bible,
The New International Version. Copyright © 1973, 1978, 1984
by the International Bible Society. Used by permission of Zondervan
Bible Publishers.

Also used is:
NASB—The New American Standard Bible © The Lockman
Foundation 1960, 1962, 1963, 1968, 1971, 1973, 1975.
Used by permission.

© Copyright 1989 by Gospel Light. All rights reserved. Printed in U.S.A.

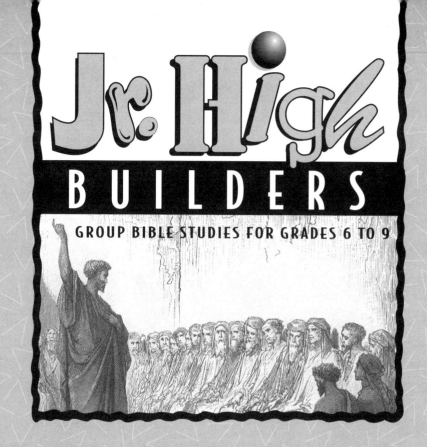

Jr. High BUILDERS

GROUP BIBLE STUDIES FOR GRADES 6 TO 9

GREAT TRUTHS FROM EPHESIANS

NUMBER 11 IN A SERIES OF 12

Gospel Light

INTRODUCTION

This book contains everything you need to teach any size group of junior high students about 12 important truths from Ephesians. Thirteen sessions, with complete session plans for the leader, reproducible classroom worksheets and reproducible take-home papers. Also included are 13 lecture-oriented Bible study outlines based on the same themes, to provide your students with needed reinforcement from a fresh perspective. And—dozens of action games and ideas to round out your youth program, plus a special section of clip art featuring illustrations to promote your Bible studies and dress up your announcement handbills.

Contents

Bible Studies

OVERVIEW
OF THE PARTS AND PIECES

There is a ton of great teaching tools in this book, including object lessons, Bible games, memory verses, discussion questions, stories, worksheets, comic cartoons and more! Here's an overview of it all:

The **SESSION PLAN** contains two essential ingredients for a meaningful Bible study all students will enjoy: a commentary section to provide the leader with important biblical information and to set the stage for the lesson; and a lesson plan filled with Bible Learning Activities to help students retain spiritual truths. **FOR A DETAILED DESCRIPTION, TURN TO PAGE 6.**

The **STUDENT WORKSHEET,** called the **Key,** allows the student to learn by doing rather than just sitting and listening. Photocopy as many sheets as you need. **SEE PAGE 8 FOR COMPLETE DETAILS.**

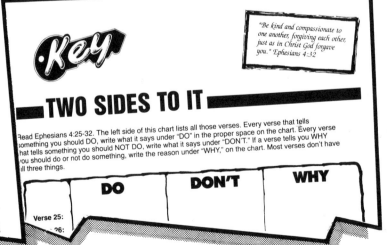

Wisdom
SESSION 2

INSIGHTS FOR THE LEADER

WHAT THE SESSION IS ABOUT
Through Christ we can live wisely.

SCRIPTURE STUDIED
Proverbs 3:5,6; Matthew 6:22,23; John 8:32; Ephesians 1:15-23; 5:15; James 1:5

KEY PASSAGE
"I keep asking that the God of our Lord Jesus Christ, the glorious Father, may give you the Spirit of revelation, so that you better."

Ephesians 1:15-23 is actually a prayer which Paul prayed for the Ephesian Christians who would read his letter. It is a beautiful prayer which skips trivialities and gets to the heart of the Ephesians' spiritual needs.

It is a good prayer for a junior high Bible study leader to pray for his or her students. When your prayers are on the level of, "God, make them shut up and sit still," this prayer can serve as an example of a caring prayer that asks God for specific blessings.

What Paul Prayed
First, Paul never stopped giving thanks for the people he had nurtured in the faith (see v. 16). He reminded his readers that he hadn't prayed once for them and then forgotten them. He kept asking that God would give them the wisdom they needed to live as His own (see v. 17). We can learn from Paul that

wisdom is to better know the Lord, which will result in being set free (see John 8:32) to grow and develop in areas that we had never thought possible. It's possible for junior highers to learn all the facts about Jesus and still not know Him. As their teacher, you can help them by continually showing that Jesus is a person who can be known here and now. Your loving them with His love will take them a big step beyond "just the facts."

In Ephesians 1:18 Paul used a phrase that is reminiscent of Christ's teaching in Matthew 6:22,23: "The eye is the lamp of the body. If your eyes are good, your whole body will be full of light. But if your eyes are bad, your whole body will be full of darkness. If then the light within you is darkness, how great is that darkness!" Jesus was clearly teaching about the same kind of inner enlightenment to which Paul was referring.

It is interesting to consider that even Christians need enlightenment and Arrival for junior highers

Key

"Be kind and compassionate to one another, forgiving each other, just as in Christ God forgave you." *Ephesians 4:32*

TWO SIDES TO IT

Read Ephesians 4:25-32. The left side of this chart lists all those verses. Every verse that tells something you should DO, write what it says under "DO" in the proper space on the chart. Every verse that tells something you should NOT DO, write what it says under "DON'T." If a verse tells you WHY you should do or not do something, write the reason under "WHY," on the chart. Most verses don't have all three things.

	DO	DON'T	WHY
Verse 25:			
26:			

4

MW01223406

The **TEACHING RESOURCE PAGE** provides special items such as short stories or case studies when required by the **Session Plan.** Most **Session Plans** have no **Teaching Resource Page.** **FOR DETAILS, SEE PAGE 9.**

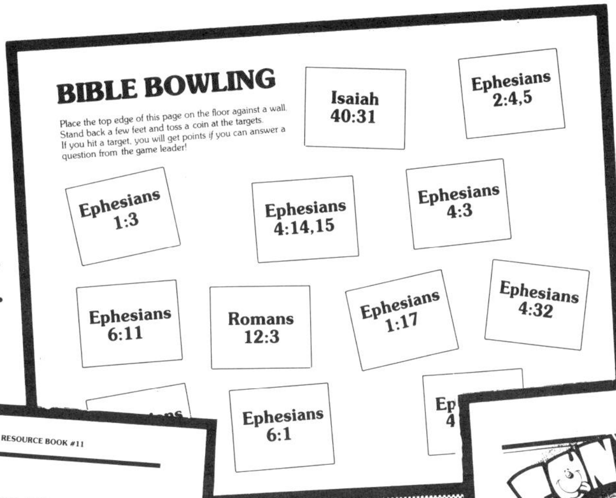

The **TAKE-HO[ME]** features a news[...] Bible game (suc[...] daily devotional [...] verse for motivated students. **FOR MORE ABOUT THE FUN PAGE, TURN TO PAGE 10.**

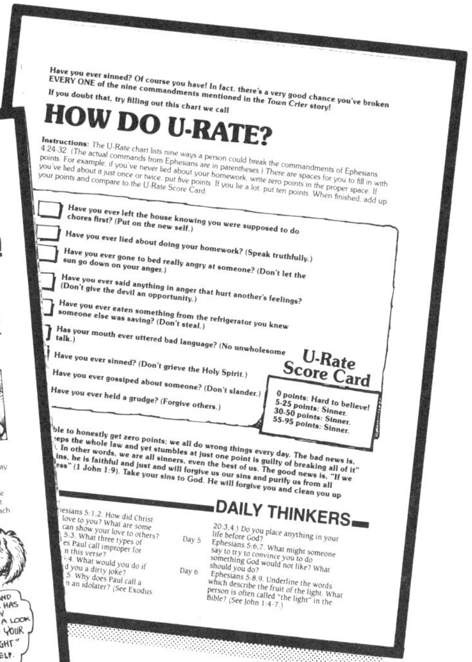

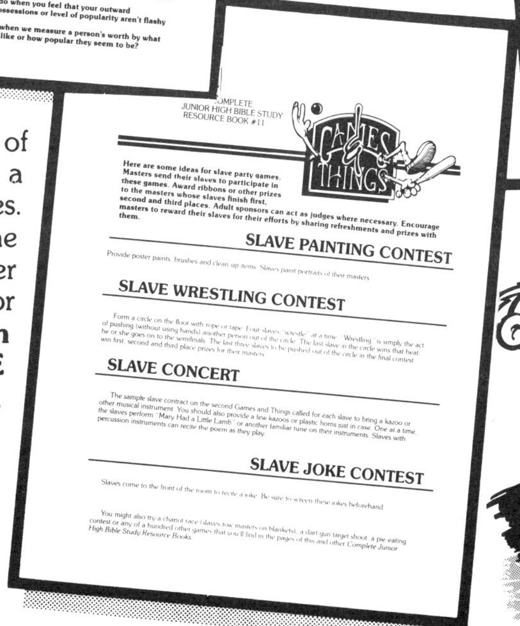

BIBLE BOWLING

Place the top edge of this page on the floor against a wall. Stand back a few feet and toss a coin at the targets. If you hit a target, you will get points *if* you can answer a question from the game leader!

Isaiah 40:31

Ephesians 2:4,5

Ephesians 1:3

Ephesians 4:14,15

Ephesians 4:3

Ephesians 6:11

Romans 12:3

Ephesians 1:17

Ephesians 4:32

Ephesians 6:1

POPSHEET
Session 4
THE COMPLETE JUNIOR HIGH BIBLE STUDY RESOURCE BOOK #11
©1989 by SSH

THEME: Self-centeredness.

BIBLE STUDY OUTLINE

Begin your message by doing the Object Lesson. Then read Luke 22:24-27 to your students. Make the following remarks as time allows.

Introductory remarks: We all have problems at times with selfishness and self-centeredness. We want to look and be like the flashy people in the flashy pictures. Would it surprise you to learn that Jesus' disciples also had the same sort of attitude?

Verse 24: It was the famous Last Supper, the meal that Jesus shared with His closest followers just hours before He was betrayed by Judas, captured by the soldiers and led off to trial and death on the cross. Somehow, during the dinner conversation, the disciples started arguing about who was the greatest among them. Can you imagine what a scene that must have been? Each person wanted to claim the credit as "Best Disciple of the Year." Maybe they thought Jesus was about to hand out trophies!

Verse 25: Jesus set them straight by telling them their behavior was like that of the unbelieving world. Those in authority loved to prideful "lord it over" their subjects. They loved to call themselves "Benefactors." History shows that then, just as now, few people in authority actually spent much time trying to benefit others. They were in it for the power, fame and loot.

Verse 26: Jesus makes it clear that things don't work that way in His spiritual kingdom. Christians are to humbly and lovingly serve one another.

Verse 27: Jesus is our example of the servant leader. He was obviously the leader of the disciples, yet He spent His time serving them in many ways. Elsewhere in the Bible (see John 13:1-17) it tells us that at this meal Jesus got down and washed His disciples' feet, a very menial task. This is the sort of Lord we have—one who cares for us and helps us.

It's not a part of human nature to want to serve others. Human nature wants to be served. But Jesus has taught us that being great means being a useful servant. Right after communicating this truth to His disciples Jesus did the greatest thing a servant could do: He gave His life for them—and for us.

OBJECT LESSON: PRETTY PICTURES

A grocery store magazine rack is a great place to find pictures of the "Beautiful People." Clip out a few photographs (after buying the magazine, of course!) featuring people who represent the world's standard of excellence: good looking people, celebrities, rich people or political leaders. Christian magazines, especially those devoted to missionary life, are a good source of pictures featuring people who serve others.

Show your students the photos, contrasting the world's favorites with the simple servants. You can ask students to point out which people seem to be the most admirable. Chances are, their choices will be wrong. Say, God doesn't look at the outside, flashy part of a human to judge his or her value. Let's take a look at a Bible passage that teaches us what God really does admire in His children.

DISCUSSION QUESTIONS

1. What are some things a junior higher could do to help and serve his or her school friends? What about at home with the family?

2. What are some ways we, as a youth group, can serve others?

3. What can you do when you feel that your outward appearance, possessions or level of popularity aren't flashy enough?

4. What happens when we measure a person's worth by what they own, look like or how popular they seem to be?

The **POPSHEET** is a lecture-oriented version of the **Session Plan,** based on a different portion of the Scriptures. Use it as an alternative to the **Session Plan,** at another meeting later in the week, or combine it with the **Session Plan** as you see fit. **SEE PAGE 12.**

The **Popsheet** features **GAMES AND THINGS,** dozens of action games, special suggestions and ideas for your students to enjoy. **PAGE 14 CONTAINS DETAILS.**

GAMES & THINGS
THE COMPLETE JUNIOR HIGH BIBLE STUDY RESOURCE BOOK #11

Here are some ideas for slave party games. Masters send their slaves to participate in these games. Award ribbons or other prizes to the masters whose slaves finish first, second and third places. Adult sponsors can act as judges where necessary. Encourage masters to reward their slaves for their efforts by sharing refreshments and prizes with them.

SLAVE PAINTING CONTEST

Provide poster paints, brushes and clean-up items. Slaves paint portraits of their masters.

SLAVE WRESTLING CONTEST

Form a circle on the floor with tape or rope. Four slaves "wrestle" at a time. Wrestling is simply the act of pushing (without using hands) another person out of the circle. The last slave in the circle wins that heat; he or she goes on to the semifinals. The last three slaves to be pushed out of the circle in the final contest win first, second and third place prizes for their masters.

SLAVE CONCERT

The sample slave contract on the second Games and Things called for each slave to bring a kazoo or other musical instrument. You should also provide a few kazoos or plastic horns just in case. One at a time, the slaves perform "Mary Had a Little Lamb" or another familiar tune on their instruments. Slaves with percussion instruments can recite the poem as they play.

SLAVE JOKE CONTEST

Slaves come to the front of the room to be a joke. Be sure to screen these jokes beforehand.

You might also try a chariot race (slaves tow masters on blankets), a dart gun target shoot, a pie eating contest or any of a hundred other games that you'll find on the pages of this and other Complete Junior High Bible Study Resource Books.

TOWN CRIER
Session 11

PERFECT FAMILY DISCOVERED!

INCREDIBLE PARENTS NEVER PUNCH, YELL AT OR MISTREAT THEIR CHILDREN!

If that's true, the Horsecollars are the only perfect family known to humankind! "Oh, it's true," claims Mr. Clyde P. Horsecollar. "My children are always happy and obedient. They cheerfully do everything I say. They always have such passive expressions on their little faces . . ." Scientists and researchers are at a loss to explain the Horsecollar family's incredible and unique happiness.

Mr. and Mrs. Horsecollar

WONDERFUL KIDS NEVER PUNCH, YELL AT OR MISTREAT THEIR PARENTS!

"We live in peace and harmony every single day," claims Doris Horsecollar. "We never fight or bicker. We are always happy. The children never disobey."

The children agree. "We love and obey our parents. It's so much fun to do our chores and to stay out of trouble," said young Jimmy Horsecollar. His sister Betsy agreed. "Mom and Dad are the greatest. They always smile and never raise their voices. It's a privilege and a pleasure to do everything they say. We love it."

When asked how they would react if their parents were to forbid their going to a party, the young Horsecollars said, "Oh, we never go out anyway. We will just sit in the living room and smile at each other."

The Younger Horsecollars

ILLEGAL TOXIC WASTE DUMP UNEARTHED!

Government scientists announced the discovery of an illegal toxic waste dump today. "The health hazards are severe," said Dr. Fishlips, local health official assigned to the investigation. "The chemicals and fumes from the dump will cause severe brain damage, including feelings of euphoria and loss of contact with reality. Anyone living within 40 yards of this site will be in a constant state of oblivion. They'll be little more than wet noodles."

Coincidentally, the toxic waste dump is located 20 yards from the house of a family also in the news, the Horsecollars.

IT'S A FAIRY TALE, ISN'T IT? NO FAMILY IS AS HAPPY AND WELL-ADJUSTED AS THE HORSECOLLARS. EVERY FAMILY GOES THROUGH TRIALS AND CONFLICTS NOW AND THEN. THE BIBLE HAS MUCH ADVICE FOR IMPROVING FAMILY RELATIONSHIPS. FOR EXAMPLE, TAKE A LOOK AT EPHESIANS 6:1— "CHILDREN, OBEY YOUR PARENTS IN THE LORD, FOR THIS IS RIGHT."

OBEYING YOUR PARENTS ALL THE TIME IS NOT ALWAYS EASY! ALLOW GOD TO HELP. PRAY. TALK TO YOUR MINISTER IF NEEDED.

Have you ever sinned? Of course you have! In fact, there's a very good chance you've broken EVERY ONE of the nine commandments mentioned in the Town Crier story!

If you doubt that, try filling out this chart we call

HOW DO U-RATE?

Instructions: The U-Rate chart lists nine ways a person could break the commandments of Ephesians 4:24-32. (The actual commands from Ephesians are in parentheses.) There are spaces for you to fill in with points. For example, if you've never lied about your homework, write zero points in the proper space. If you've lied about it just once or twice, put five points. If you lie a lot, put ten points. When finished, add up your points and compare to the U-Rate Score Card.

- [ ] Have you ever left the house knowing you were supposed to do chores first? (Put on the new self.)
- [ ] Have you ever lied about doing your homework? (Speak truthfully.)
- [ ] Have you ever gone to bed really angry at someone? (Don't let the sun go down on your anger.)
- [ ] Have you ever said anything in anger that hurt another's feelings? (Don't give the devil an opportunity.)
- [ ] Have you ever eaten something from the refrigerator you knew someone else was saving? (Don't steal.)
- [ ] Has your mouth ever uttered bad language? (No unwholesome talk.)
- [ ] Have you ever sinned? (Don't grieve the Holy Spirit.)
- [ ] Have you ever gossiped about someone? (Don't slander.)
- [ ] Have you ever held a grudge? (Forgive others.)

U-Rate Score Card

If you're able to honestly get zero points, we all do wrong things every day. The bad news is that nobody keeps the whole law and we all stumble at just one point is guilty of breaking all of it. In other words, we are all sinners, even the best of us. The good news is, "If we confess our sins, he is faithful and just and will forgive us our sins and purify us from all unrighteousness" (1 John 1:9). Take your sins to God. He will forgive you and clean you up.

0 points: Hard to believe!
5-25 points: Sinner.
30-50 points: Sinner.
55-95 points: Sinner.

DAILY THINKERS

Ephesians 5:1,2. How did Christ show His love to you? What are some ways you can show your love to others?

Ephesians 5:3. What three types of sins are Paul call improper for use in this verse?

Ephesians 5:4. What would you do if you a dirty joke?

Ephesians 5:5. Why does Paul call a person an idolater? (See Exodus 20:3,4.)

Day 5

Ephesians 5:6,7. What might someone say to try to convince you to do something God would not like? What should you do?

Day 6

Ephesians 5:8,9. Underline the words which describe the fruit of the light. What person is often called "the light" in the Bible? (See John 1:4-7.)

The **CLIP ART AND OTHER GOODIES** section at the back of the book contains special art you can use to dress up your newsletters. **SEE PAGE 16 FOR COMPLETE INFORMATION.**

RIVER TRIP

JESUS IS KING!

THE SESSION PLANS

How to squeeze the most out of each Bible study.

● Every Session Plan contains the following features:

1. INTRODUCTORY INFORMATION

WHAT THE SESSION IS ABOUT states the main thrust of the lesson.

Your students will examine all verses listed in **SCRIPTURE STUDIED**.

The **KEY PASSAGE** is also the memory verse given on the **Key** student worksheet (when space allows) and the **Fun Page** take-home paper.

AIMS OF THE SESSION are what you hope to achieve during class time. You may wish to privately review these after class as a measure of your success.

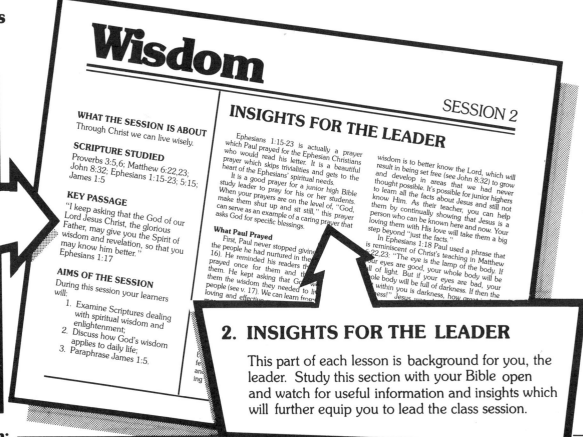

Wisdom

SESSION 2

WHAT THE SESSION IS ABOUT
Through Christ we can live wisely.

SCRIPTURE STUDIED
Proverbs 3:5,6; Matthew 6:22,23; John 8:32; Ephesians 1:15-23; 5:15; James 1:5

KEY PASSAGE
"I keep asking that the God of our Lord Jesus Christ, the glorious Father, may give you the Spirit of wisdom and revelation, so that you may know him better."
Ephesians 1:17

AIMS OF THE SESSION
During this session your learners will:
1. Examine Scriptures dealing with spiritual wisdom and enlightenment;
2. Discuss how God's wisdom applies to daily life;
3. Paraphrase James 1:5.

INSIGHTS FOR THE LEADER

Ephesians 1:15-23 is actually a prayer which Paul prayed for the Ephesian Christians who would read his letter. It is a beautiful prayer which skips trivialities and gets to the heart of the Ephesians' spiritual needs.
It is a good prayer for a junior high Bible study leader to pray for his or her students. When your prayers are on the level of, "God, make them shut up and sit still," this prayer can serve as an example of a caring prayer that asks God for specific blessings.

What Paul Prayed
First, Paul never stopped giving [thanks for] the people he had nurtured in the[ir faith] (v. 16). He reminded his readers th[at he] prayed once for them and the[n for] them. He kept asking that Go[d would give] them the wisdom they needed to li[ve as] people (see v. 17). We can learn fro[m this] loving and effective [prayer...]

wisdom is to better know the Lord, which will result in being set free (see John 8:32) to grow and develop in areas that we had never thought possible. It's possible for junior highers to learn all the facts about Jesus and still not know Him. As their teacher, you can help them by continually showing that Jesus is a person who can be known here and now. Your loving them with His love will take them a big step beyond "just the facts."
In Ephesians 1:18 Paul used a phrase that is reminiscent of Christ's teaching in Matthew [6:]22,23: "The eye is the lamp of the body. If [yo]ur eyes are good, your whole body will be [fu]ll of light. But if your eyes are bad, your [wh]ole body will be full of darkness. If then the [light] within you is darkness, how great [is that darkn]ess!" Jesus was...

2. INSIGHTS FOR THE LEADER

This part of each lesson is background for you, the leader. Study this section with your Bible open and watch for useful information and insights which will further equip you to lead the class session.

 Things to note about the Session Plan:

The **Session Plan** makes heavy use of **Bible Learning Activities**. A Bible Learning Activity (BLA) is precisely what it sounds like—an activity students perform to learn about the Bible. Because action is employed, the student has a much greater chance of **comprehending** and **retaining** spiritual insights. And because you, the leader, can see what the student is doing—whether it's a written assignment, skit or art activity—you can readily **measure** the student's comprehension. The BLA allows you to **walk about the classroom** as students work, answering questions or dealing with problem students. Furthermore, it's **easier to teach well** using BLAs. If you've never used BLAs before, you will quickly find them much simpler to prepare and deliver than a whole session of lecture.

The **Session Plan** provides guided conversation—suggestions on what to say throughout the class time. Notice that the guided conversation is always printed in **bold type** in the **Session Plan.** Regular light type indicates instructions to you, the teacher.

3. SESSION PLAN

This heading introduces the step-by-step lesson plan. With careful planning, you can easily tailor each session to the amount of class time you have

4. BEFORE CLASS BEGINS

This is a convenient list of any special preparation or materials required.

5. ATTENTION GRABBER

Who knows what lurks in the minds of your students as they file into your room? The **Attention Grabber** will stimulate their interest and focus their thinking on the theme of the lesson.

The **Attention Grabber,** as well as other parts of the **Session Plan,** often—but not always—contain an additional alternate activity. These alternates are identified by the titles **CREATIVE OPTION, OPTIONAL** or similar designations. Choose the activity that best suits the needs of your class and fits your time schedule.

6. BIBLE EXPLORATION

The **Bible Exploration** is the heart of your class session because it involves each learner directly in the study of God's Word. It is during this period that you will invite the students to explore and discover **what the Bible says and means** and to discuss **how it applies to each student.**

SESSION PLAN

BEFORE CLASS BEGINS: Now is a good time to check to see if your classroom has all the materials listed under "Necessary Classroom Supplies" on page 7. It is essential that students have Bibles. Be sure to provide extras for those students who do not bring a Bible. Photocopy Teaching Resource page crossword puzzle (enough for each pair of students to have one) and Fun Page take-home paper. There is no Key student worksheet this time. See the ATTENT GRABBER and CONCLUSION for special preparation. Step 3 of the EXPLORATION calls large sheet of butcher paper to be fastened to the classroom wall—it's best to do that before dents arrive.

Attention Grabber

ATTENTION GRABBER (5-7 minutes)

Before class, write the word "blessings" on sheets of paper—one large letter per sheet. Hide the letters in various parts of the room.

As students arrive, invite them to figure out the subject of today's session by finding the nine hidden letters and piecing the word back together.

When the students have succeeded at their task,

say something like this: **Many of us have a n** easier time thinking about the bad thing happen to us rather than the good thing God has provided. Let's see if we can m change and take a closer look at what G has done for us and what He is continui do.

Bible Exploration

EXPLORATION (35-45 minutes)

Materials needed: Step 3 involves students in creating a graffiti poster. Fasten butcher paper along a classroom wall, enough paper so that the entire class can gather before it to write. Provide marking pens. If you trust your students not to make a mess, you can also let some of them use spray paint and

spray glitter to give the poster some flair.

Step 1 (15-20 minutes): Explain, **We ar beginning a study in the New Testame of Ephesians. This was a letter writter apostle Paul. He was in prison in Ron waiting for a hearing before Nero, wh**

---

7. CONCLUSION AND DECISION

Each **Session Plan** provides this opportunity for students to deal with the questions, **What does the Bible mean to me? How can I put what I just learned into practice in my own life?** Be sure to leave enough time at the end of each session for the **Conclusion and Decision** activity.

8. NOTES

Every page of the **Session Plan** allows space for you to jot notes as you prepare for class. Also, you will find **important reminders** and **suggestions** listed in **bold type** to catch your attention.

NECESSARY CLASSROOM SUPPLIES

The Session Plan Bible study activities require that you make the following items readily available to students:

• A Bible for each student (Essential!) • Paper and pencils or pens • Felt markers • Butcher paper for posters • Transparent tape • Scissors

You will need a chalkboard and chalk, or overhead projector, transparencies and transparency markers.

Special requirements will be listed in the proper **Session Plans.**

THE KEY
STUDENT WORKSHEETS
The Key helps students unlock Bible truths.

The page immediately following most **Session Plans** is the **Key** worksheet for your students. Here's how to use the **Key**:

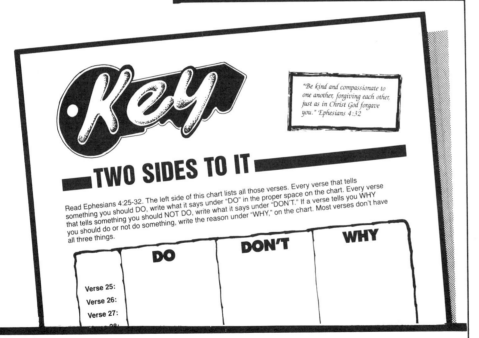

1. Before class, photocopy enough student worksheets for your learners and a few extra for visitors. There is never more than one **Key** worksheet per session—some sessions have none at all.

2. The **Keys** are generally used throughout each **Session Plan.** The best time to distribute them to students is when the **Session Plan** first calls for their use. Always keep a copy for yourself.

3. Be sure to have plenty of blank paper for students' written assignments—the **Keys** don't have much extra space.

4. It may help to have your students fold their **Key** into their Bibles if there is a gap between uses of the worksheet. This will aid you in avoiding the dreaded Paper Airplane Syndrome!

5. Collect and save the worksheets once every few weeks. (Do not collect worksheets that contain private confessions to God or the like.) You can follow the progress of your students by examining their work. Parents, too, will want to see what their kids are learning.

Each session's Key features that session's memory verse (which is also printed on the Fun Page take-home paper). If you have a little extra time at the end of the lesson, review the memory verse with your students.

THE TEACHING RESOURCE PAGES

Special goodies to help you teach.

A few sessions require extra teaching tools such as board games or scrambled Bible verses. These are provided by the **Teaching Resource Pages** which follow the **Key** student worksheet in the appropriate sessions.

The **Session Plans** and the **Teaching Resource Pages** contain complete instructions.

BIBLE BOWLING GAME LEADER'S SHEET

When a player's coin lands on one of the passages listed below, read that passage aloud and ask one of the simple questions listed with the passage. If the player can answer the question, award him or her the appropriate number of points and record the points on the Score Card. Be sure to discuss the significance of the truths the players are looking at. Add any of your own insights. Play until the class leader calls time.

POINTS: The last number of each reference is the points that passage is worth. For example, Ephesians 1:3 is worth three points, Isaiah 40:31 is worth one point and so on.

QUESTIONS: It's OK to ask the same question more than once—this will help players retain the information. Feel free, however, to make up your own questions. Also, when a player correctly answers a question, offer bonus points if he or she can provide more information. For example, if a player can remember one or two of the actual spiritual blessings alluded to in Ephesians 1:3, award 10 points. You'll need your Bible to check on the answers. (Note: INSIGHTS FOR THE LEADER in Session 1 details the spiritual blessings alluded to in Ephesians 1:3, as do verses 4-14 of the first chapter of Ephesians.)

ISAIAH 40:31

"But those who hope in the Lord will renew their strength. They will soar on wings like eagles; they will run and not grow weary, they will walk and not be faint."

1. What do we have to do to renew our spiritual strength? (Hope in the Lord.)
2. Name two of the things that will happen if you place your hope in the Lord. (Renew strength, soar, run without growing tired, walk and not faint.)

ROMANS 12:3

"For by the grace given me I say to every one of you: Do not think of yourself more highly than you ought, but rather think of yourself with sober judgment, in accordance with the measure of faith God has given you."

1. How are we not to think of ourselves? (More highly than we should.)
2. How are we to think of ourselves? (With sober judgment.)

EPHESIANS 1:3

"Praise be to the God and Father of our Lord Jesus Christ, who has blessed us in the heavenly realms with every spiritual blessing in Christ."

1. What have we been blessed with? (Spiritual blessings.)
2. Whom do we have to be in to be blessed? (Christ.)

EPHESIANS 1:17

"I keep asking that the God of our Lord Jesus Christ, the glorious Father, may give you the Spirit of wisdom and revelation, so that you may know him better."

1. Paul prays that God will give us the Spirit of what? (Wisdom and revelation.)
2. We should have the Spirit of wisdom and revelation so that we may do what? (Know God better.)

EPHESIANS 2:4,5

"But because of his great love for us, God, who is rich in mercy, made us alive with Christ even when we were dead in transgressions—it is by grace you have been saved."

1. What have we been made? (Alive with Christ.)
2. We used to be dead in what? (Transgressions.)

EPHESIANS 4:3

"Make every effort to keep the unity of the Spirit through the bond of peace."

1. What are we to strive to keep? (Unity of the Spirit.)
2. We are to keep the unity of God's Spirit through what? (Peace.)

THE FUN PAGE
TAKE-HOME PAPERS

Give your students a treat! The Fun Page combines games, cartoons, short stories, memory verses and daily devotional studies into an enjoyable, fun-filled take-home paper.

Features:

Each **Fun Page** is designed to amplify the insights gained in the classroom. The **Fun Page** has a newspaper motif, with a set of cartoon reporters who attempt to dig out the truth about each session's subject.

Session 11

TOWN CRIER
PERFECT FAMILY DISCOVERED!

INCREDIBLE PARENTS NEVER PUNCH, YELL AT OR MISTREAT THEIR CHILDREN!

"We live in peace and harmony every single day," claims Mr. Clyde P. Horsecollar. "We never fight or bicker. We are always happy. The children never disobey."

Mr. and Mrs. Horsecollar

If that's true, the Horsecollars are the only perfect family known to humankind!

"Oh, it's true," said Doris Horsecollar. "My children are always happy and obedient. They cheerfully do everything I say. They always have such passive expressions on their little faces."

Scientists and researchers are at a loss to explain the Horsecollar family's incredible and unique happiness.

WONDERFUL KIDS NEVER PUNCH, YELL AT OR MISTREAT THEIR PARENTS!

"We love and obey our parents. It's so much fun to do our chores and to stay out of trouble." So said young Jimmy Horsecollar. His sister Betsy agreed: "Mom and Dad are the greatest. They

The Younger Horsecollars

always smile and never raise their voices. It's a privilege and a pleasure to do everything they say. We love it."

When asked how they would react if their parents were to forbid their going to a party, the young Horsecollars said, "Oh, we never go out. We all just sit in the living room and smile at each other."

ILLEGAL TOXIC WASTE DUMP UNEARTHED!

Government scientists announced the discovery of an illegal toxic waste dump today.

"The health hazards are severe," said Dr. Fishlips, local health official assigned to the investigation. "The chemicals and fumes from the dump will cause severe brain damage, including feelings of euphoria and loss of contact with reality. Anyone living within 40 yards of this site will be in a constant state of oblivion. They'll be little more than wet noodles."

Coincidentally, the toxic waste dump is located 20 yards from the house of a family also in the news, the Horsecollars.

IT'S A FAIRY TALE, ISN'T IT? NO FAMILY IS AS HAPPY AND WELL-ADJUSTED AS THE HORSECOLLARS. EVERY FAMILY GOES THROUGH TRIALS AND CONFLICTS NOW AND THEN. THE BIBLE HAS MUCH ADVICE FOR IMPROVING FAMILY RELATIONSHIPS. FOR EXAMPLE, TAKE A LOOK AT EPHESIANS 6:1— "CHILDREN, OBEY YOUR PARENTS IN THE LORD, FOR THIS IS RIGHT." ULP!! NOT ALWAYS EASY! ALLOW GOD TO HELP. PRAY. TALK TO YOUR MINISTER IF NEEDED.

Have you ever sinned? Of course you have! In fact, there's a very good chance you've broken EVERY ONE of the nine commandments mentioned in the *Town Crier* story!

If you doubt that, try filling out this chart we call

HOW DO U-RATE?

Instructions: The U-Rate chart lists nine ways a person could break the commandments of Ephesians 4:24-32. (The actual commands from Ephesians are in parentheses.) There are spaces for you to fill in with points. For example, if you've never lied about your homework, write zero points in the proper space. If you've lied about it just once or twice, put five points. If you lie a lot, put ten points. When finished, add up your points and compare to the U-Rate Score Card.

☐ Have you ever left the house knowing you were supposed to do chores first? (Put on the new self.)

☐ Have you ever lied about doing your homework? (Speak truthfully.)

☐ Have you ever gone to bed really angry at someone? (Don't let the sun go down on your anger.)

☐ Have you ever said anything in anger that hurt another's feelings? (Don't give the devil an opportunity.)

☐ Have you ever eaten something from the refrigerator you knew someone else was saving? (Don't steal.)

☐ Has your mouth ever uttered bad language? (No unwholesome talk.)

☐ Have you ever sinned? (Don't grieve the Holy Spirit.)

☐ Have you ever gossiped about someone? (Don't slander.)

☐ Have you ever held a grudge? (Forgive others.)

U-Rate Score Card

0 points: Hard to believe!
5-25 points: Sinner.
30-50 points: Sinner.
55-95 points: Sinner.

It's impossible to honestly get zero points; we all do wrong things every day. The bad news is, "Whoever keeps the whole law and yet stumbles at just one point is guilty of breaking all of it" (James 2:10). In other words, we are all sinners, even the best of us. The good news is, "If we confess our sins, he is faithful and just and will forgive us our sins and purify us from all unrighteousness" (1 John 1:9). Take your sins to God. He will forgive you and clean you up again!

DAILY THINKERS

Day 1   Read Ephesians 5:1,2. How did Christ show His love to you? What are some ways you can show your love to others?

Day 2   Ephesians 5:3. What three types of conduct does Paul call improper for Christians in this verse?

Day 3   Ephesians 5:4. What would you do if someone told you a dirty joke?

Day 4   Ephesians 5:5. Why does Paul call a greedy person an idolater? (See Exodus

20:3,4.) Do you place anything in your life before God?

Day 5   Ephesians 5:6,7. What might someone say to try to convince you to do something God would not like? What should you do?

Day 6   Ephesians 5:8,9. Underline the words which describe the fruit of the light. What person is often called "the light" in the Bible? (See John 1:4-7.)

You'll also find Bible games that your students will love: mazes, crosswords, word searches—games ranging from the simple to the extremely challenging. Again, they are all designed to reinforce what the students have learned during the session time.

The **Daily Thinkers** section is a simple six-day devotional based on passages related to the Scriptures studied in class.

Today's Good News memory verse helps students lock the wisdom of God's Word into their minds and hearts.

How to Use the **Fun Page:**

Photocopy both sides of the **Fun Page** back-to-back, just as it appears in this manual. (If your copy machine cannot do this, we suggest you copy each side on a separate sheet.) Make enough copies for your students plus a few extras for visitors. Note: You may like to occasionally save the **Fun Page** game for use during another Bible study time.

You can use the **Fun Page** several ways:

As a **take-home paper** to extend the classroom into the week. Hand out copies as students leave class.

As a special **Bible Learning Activity** during class. (Some of the games would make interesting **Attention Grabbers,** for example.)

Make it the **focal point of another Bible study.** For instance, if you used the **Session Plan** Sunday morning, you could reinforce the lesson during an informal midweek meeting by involving students in answering the questions in the **Daily Thinkers.**

Even absentees can be involved. Put the **Fun Page** into an envelope along with a personal note to that learner who needs a little encouragement.

THE POPSHEET
LECTURE BIBLE STUDIES

"Pop" these **Popsheets** out of this book and give them to the leader of your youth group's other meetings. Great for an at-home Bible study, a camp retreat, games night or special event.

Youth groups come in all sizes and shapes. So do youth programs. Meetings vary widely in style—ranging from Sunday morning Bible studies with singing and announcements, to deeper discipleship programs for motivated students, to the fun and action of game nights with very short Bible messages.

The **Popsheets** offer a good source of creative thinking for whatever type of program you have. **Popsheets** are packed with Bible stories, object lessons, case studies, discussion questions and fast-paced games and other ideas aimed at the junior high "squirrel" mentality! Each **Popsheet** covers the same basic theme as the accompanying **Session Plan,** but the stories, verses, object lessons and case studies are all new and fresh.

The advantages?

● For students who attended the **Session Plan** class, a fresh new perspective on the topic. A great way to insure retention.

● For learners who missed the **Session Plan** class, a good way to keep current with the other students. This is a sound method to guarantee that all your youth group members explore every topic in a Bible study series.

● Or use your creativity to replace some of the Bible Learning Activities in the **Session Plans** with object lessons and short stories from the **Popsheets.**

THEME

Roughly the same theme as the accompanying **Session Plan**.

BIBLE STUDY OUTLINE

A suggested Bible passage with a list of important points to make during your lecture, the **Bible Study Outline** offers a *basic* lesson plan to stimulate your thinking as you prayerfully prepare your message. **Use your own creativity and ability to "flesh it out."** There is plenty here to help you create outstanding Bible messages your students will enjoy and remember.

Notice that the **Bible Study Outline** contains no **Bible Learning Activities.** The **Popsheet** is designed to be a short Bible message (five to ten minutes) that you can give at an informal games night, camp cabin devotional, or similar setting.

OBJECT LESSON

Each **Popsheet** has an object lesson, short story or case study. (A case study is a description of an event or situation a junior high student is likely to face in life.) These add spice to your messages. A good object lesson, for instance, and the spiritual truth it conveys, can be remembered for a lifetime.

THE COMPLETE JUNIOR HIGH BIBLE STUDY RESOURCE BOOK #11
©1989 by SSH.

Session 4

THEME: Self-centeredness.

BIBLE STUDY OUTLINE

Begin your message by doing the Object Lesson. Then read Luke 22:24-27 to your students. Make the following remarks as time allows.

Introductory remarks: We all have problems at times with selfishness and self-centeredness. We want to look and be like the flashy people in the flashy pictures. Would it surprise you to learn that Jesus' disciples also had the same sort of attitude?

Verse 24: It was the famous Last Supper, the meal that Jesus shared with His closest followers just hours before He was betrayed by Judas, captured by the soldiers and led off to trial and death on the cross. Somehow, during the dinner conversation, the disciples started arguing about who was the greatest among them. Can you imagine what a scene that must have been? Each person wanted to claim the credit as "Best Disciple of the Year." Maybe they thought Jesus was about to hand out trophies!

Verse 25: Jesus set them straight by telling them their behavior was like that of the unbelieving world. Those in authority loved to pridefully "lord it over" their subjects. They loved to call themselves "Benefactors." History shows that then, just as now, few people in authority actually spent much time trying to benefit others. They were in it for the power, fame and loot.

Verse 26: Jesus makes it clear that things don't work that way in His spiritual kingdom. Christians are to humbly and lovingly serve one another.

Verse 27: Jesus is our example of the servant-leader. He was obviously the leader of the disciples, yet He spent His time serving them in many ways. Elsewhere in the Bible (see John 13:1-17) it tells us that at this meal Jesus got down and washed His disciples' feet, a very menial task. This is the sort of Lord we have—one who cares for us and helps us.

It's not a part of human nature to want to serve others. Human nature wants to be served. But Jesus has taught us that being great means being a useful servant. Right after communicating this truth to His disciples Jesus did the greatest thing a servant could do. He gave His life for them—and for us.

OBJECT LESSON: PRETTY PICTURES

A grocery store magazine rack is a great place to find pictures of the "Beautiful People." Clip out a few photographs (after buying the magazine, of course!) featuring people who represent the world's standard of excellence: good-looking people, celebrities, rich people or political leaders. Christian magazines, especially those devoted to missionary life, are a good source of pictures featuring people who serve others.

Show your students the photos, contrasting the world's favorites with the simple servants. You can ask students to point out which people seem to be the most admirable. Chances are, their choices will be wrong. Say, **God doesn't look at the outside, flashy part of a human to judge his or her value. Let's take a look at a Bible passage that teaches us what God really does admire in His children.**

DISCUSSION QUESTIONS

1. What are some things a junior higher could do to help and serve his or her school friends? What about at home with the family?

2. What are some ways we, as a youth group, can serve others?

3. What can you do when you feel that your outward appearance, possessions or level of popularity aren't flashy enough?

4. What happens when we measure a person's worth by what they own, look like or how popular they seem to be?

DISCUSSION QUESTIONS

You may wish to involve your students in your lectures by asking them about the issues and implications of the Bible study. Feel free to modify or add to the questions to more nearly suit your students' needs.

The **Popsheet** is intended to be folded and placed in a Bible for easy reference as the leader teaches.

GAMES AND THINGS

THE COMPLETE
JUNIOR HIGH BIBLE STUDY
RESOURCE BOOK #11

Here are some ideas for slave party games. Masters send their slaves to participate in these games. Award ribbons or other prizes to the masters whose slaves finish first, second and third places. Adult sponsors can act as judges where necessary. Encourage masters to reward their slaves for their efforts by sharing refreshments and prizes with them.

SLAVE PAINTING CONTEST

Provide poster paints, brushes and clean-up items. Slaves paint portraits of their masters.

SLAVE WRESTLING CONTEST

Form a circle on the floor with rope or tape. Four slaves "wrestle" at a time. "Wrestling" is simply the act of pushing (without using hands) another person out of the circle. The last slave in the circle wins that heat; he or she goes on to the semifinals. The last three slaves to be pushed out of the circle in the final contest win first, second and third place prizes for their masters.

SLAVE CONCERT

The sample slave contract on the second Games and Things called for each slave to bring a kazoo or other musical instrument. You should also provide a few kazoos or plastic horns just in case. One at a time, the slaves perform "Mary Had a Little Lamb" or another familiar tune on their instruments. Slaves with percussion instruments can recite the poem as they play.

SLAVE JOKE CONTEST

Slaves come to the front of the room to recite a joke. Be sure to screen these jokes beforehand.

You might also try a chariot race (slaves tow masters on blankets), a dart gun target shoot, a pie-eating contest or any of a hundred other games that you'll find in the pages of this and other *Complete Junior High Bible Study Resource Books*.

On the reverse side of the **Popsheet** you will find **Games and Things,** a wonderful collection of:

1. Action activities for your games night, youth group activities, socials, youth Vacation Bible Schools, camps— wherever kids are gathered. Give a copy to the leader of the games night program; he or she will love you for it!

2. Creative suggestions for social events, community involvement and the like.

3. Paper games similar to the **Fun Page** games—Use them as the focal point of an at-home style Bible study for a nice change of pace.

4. Special ideas such as posters (which you can enlarge on a copy machine or opaque projector). These special ideas will appear occasionally in this and future **Junior High Bible Study Resource Books.**

EXCITING OPTIONS FOR THE SMALL YOUTH PROGRAM

Mix and match: Putting together a customized class time tailored to *your* students.

We hope that by reading these introductory pages you've come to realize how hard we are working to bring you a truly useful resource manual for your youth program. There is plenty here for your Sunday School classes, midweek Bible studies, games meetings and special events—even if you do all these things every week.

But what do you do with all these ideas if you're a small congregation with no youth staff (or one poor overworked "volunteer")? This is where **The Complete Junior High Bible Study Resource Book** really shines. By spending a few hours each week in preparation, you can mix and match the best features of each **Session Plan, Decoder, Key, Popsheet** and **Games and Things** to build a wonderful classroom experience for your students. This illustration gives you some idea of the scope available to you:

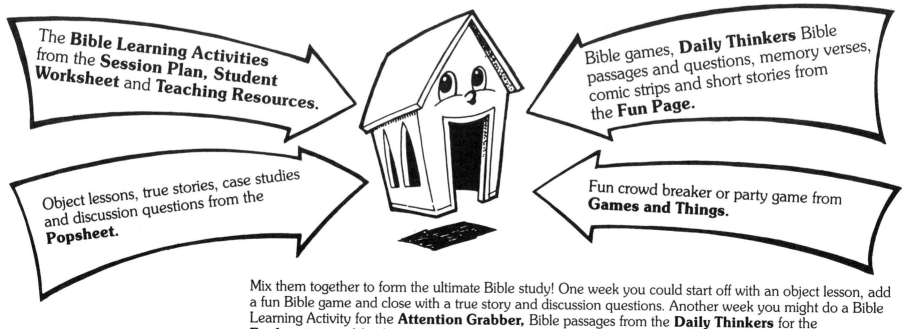

The **Bible Learning Activities** from the **Session Plan, Student Worksheet** and **Teaching Resources.**

Bible games, **Daily Thinkers** Bible passages and questions, memory verses, comic strips and short stories from the **Fun Page.**

Object lessons, true stories, case studies and discussion questions from the **Popsheet.**

Fun crowd breaker or party game from **Games and Things.**

Mix them together to form the ultimate Bible study! One week you could start off with an object lesson, add a fun Bible game and close with a true story and discussion questions. Another week you might do a Bible Learning Activity for the **Attention Grabber,** Bible passages from the **Daily Thinkers** for the **Exploration** and finish with a party to celebrate God's provision. Each week can be a new and exciting experience that your students will look forward to.

INTRODUCTION TO CLIP ART

Good news for those who can't draw.

If you want your class or youth group to increase in size—and who doesn't— you'll welcome the **Clip Art and Other Goodies** section found at the rear of this book. Create your own terrific monthly youth group activity calendars, announcement sheets and posters. It's fun and easy! Simply follow the tips and techniques in the **Clip Art and Other Goodies** section; you'll produce great "promo pieces" that will attract kids to your Bible studies and other events.

Remember: Even if you can't draw cartoons, with the right promotional clip art you can draw kids!

WHAT THE SESSION IS ABOUT
God has given us spiritual blessings in Christ.

SCRIPTURE STUDIED
Ephesians 1:1-14

KEY PASSAGE
"Praise be to the God and Father of our Lord Jesus Christ, who has blessed us in the heavenly realms with every spiritual blessing in Christ." Ephesians 1:3

AIMS OF THE SESSION
During this session your learners will:
1. Study the blessings Paul listed in his salutation to the Ephesians;
2. Identify spiritual and material blessings received by Christians;
3. Praise God for His blessings.

INSIGHTS FOR THE LEADER

While the apostle Paul was imprisoned in Rome for his preaching about Jesus, he wrote several letters to churches for which he had a special concern. Ephesians is one of those warm "prison letters." In it Paul wrote about the greatness of Christ and the salvation He offers, and the practical outcome of that salvation in the everyday lives of Christians.

Paul and Ephesus
Paul had spent a total of about three years in Ephesus, a Gentile city in Asia Minor (now Turkey) and an important trading center. He first visited there briefly (see Acts 18:19-21) and had discussions with Jews in the synagogue. Later he returned to Ephesus (see Acts 19) and encountered much conflict with both the Jews and the adherents of pagan religions. There was a riot over Christianity's threat to the worship of Artemis, a Roman goddess whose temple was in Ephesus. Paul later wrote that he "fought wild beasts in Ephesus" (1 Corinthians 15:32). This phrase is generally thought to be a dramatic figure of speech referring to Paul's conflict with ungodly men who tried to stop him from preaching the gospel.

On his way to Jerusalem, where he was sure he would be arrested and perhaps killed, Paul stopped at Miletus and sent for the church elders from Ephesus (see Acts 20:16-38). He gave them a tender good-bye and prayed with them. Acts 21:1 tells us that Paul and his traveling companions had to tear themselves away from the Ephesian elders, so great was their affection for this man who had brought Christ to them.

Blessings for Christians
The letter begins with a greeting to the "saints"—a word meaning not a select few who have special standing with God, but "set apart ones" made holy in Jesus Christ. Paul then goes into a lavish description of the blessings God has given to Christians. The paragraph is almost overwhelming; at best it's hard to take in everything Paul meant to say. Each blessing is almost beyond belief, beyond description. It's hard enough for adults to appreciate the catalog of benefits which Paul sets forth. How can your junior highers get anything out of Paul's enthusiastic but often abstract writing?

To help prevent the "over their heads" or the "in one ear and out the other" syndrome, here are examples of what some of the spiritual blessings "in the heavenly realms" (Ephesians 1:3) can mean in your junior highers' lives.

Chosen in Christ
Paul states, "He [God] chose us in him [Christ]" (v. 4) and "In him we were also chosen" (v. 11). Many junior high students feel unchosen. Somebody else is always more popular, gets all the breaks, is liked by the

teachers, is better at sports or gets better grades. Whatever the junior higher longs for, some more capable and popular student gets first. You can safely assume that all your students have felt left out at some time. But God hasn't left them out! He personally chose each of them—not through a popularity contest, but because He loves them and wants them as part of His family.

Holy and Blameless

"He chose us . . . to be holy and blameless in his sight" (v. 4). Some junior highers blame themselves for not quite measuring up. Pressures of parents and school, and self-imposed pressures based on unachievable goals, media fantasy or false guilt, make them feel they are of value only if they can do well at certain things. All too easily they can carry this idea over to Christianity. But it is a false idea. The truth is, as Christians, they don't have to work at earning God's approval. He sees them as holy and blameless in Christ! The junior high Christian's nagging sense of "not quite making it" is not God's point of view.

Adopted as Children

We are "adopted as his sons" (v. 5). In your classroom you are likely to have young people from single–parent families. As divorce and remarriage have unfortunately become more and more "normal," many young people don't know exactly who they are or where they fit in their reconstructed families. If they are in Christ they are God's children, no matter what the circumstances of their human families. God is their Father who will never leave them and never change—especially in His love for them.

Forgiven of Sins

We have "the forgiveness of sins" (v. 7). Although it may seem that many junior highers cheerfully ignore God's Word and fly paper airplanes during crucial points of your lesson, they are bothered by guilt. Their consciences nag them when they've done wrong or when your lesson hits too close to home—in fact, that's one of the things that can trigger paper airplane flights! Add that futile "never quite making it" feeling and you have loads of guilt on your junior highers. God's forgiveness speaks to them then. They can be forgiven completely in Christ, cleansed by His blood and free of both real and false guilt.

The Mystery of His Will

According to verses 9 and 10, God has made known to us a mystery, and the mystery is that there will come a time when all things in heaven and on earth will be brought together under the rule of Jesus Christ.

The phrase, "bring . . . under one head" was often used of adding up a column of figures. Paul was saying that someday Jesus will cause everything to "add up" or make sense to those of us who live in such a confusing world. Jesus will be in visible charge and He will cause everything to work together in a meaningful, harmonious way.

SESSION PLAN

BEFORE CLASS BEGINS: Now is a good time to check to see if your classroom has all the materials listed under "Necessary Classroom Supplies" on page 7. It is essential that students have Bibles. Be sure to provide extras for those students who do not bring a Bible. Photocopy the Teaching Resource page crossword puzzle (enough for each pair of students to have one) and the Fun Page take-home paper. There is no Key student worksheet this time. See the ATTENTION GRABBER and CONCLUSION for special preparation. Step 3 of the EXPLORATION calls for a large sheet of butcher paper to be fastened to the classroom wall—it's best to do that before students arrive.

Attention Grabber

ATTENTION GRABBER (5-7 minutes)

Before class, write the word "blessings" on sheets of paper—one large letter per sheet. Hide the letters in various parts of the room.

As students arrive, invite them to figure out the subject of today's session by finding the nine hidden letters and piecing the word back together.

When the students have succeeded at their task, say something like this: **Many of us have a much easier time thinking about the bad things that happen to us rather than the good things that God has provided. Let's see if we can make a change and take a closer look at what God has done for us and what He is continuing to do.**

Bible Exploration

EXPLORATION (35-45 minutes)

Materials needed: Step 3 involves students in creating a graffiti poster. Fasten butcher paper along a classroom wall, enough paper so that the entire class can gather before it to write. Provide marking pens. If you trust your students not to make a mess, you can also let some of them use spray paint and spray glitter to give the poster some flair.

Step 1 (15-20 minutes): Explain, **We are beginning a study in the New Testament book of Ephesians. This was a letter written by the apostle Paul. He was in prison in Rome, waiting for a hearing before Nero, who was**

NOTES

the Caesar or emperor at that time. He wrote to the Christians in the city of Ephesus—a city in which he had earlier spent more than two years preaching the good news of Jesus Christ. As we spend time together studying this letter, we will be tapping into some of the wisdom and help that God has for us in His Word.

Ask students to get together in pairs to work the Teaching Resource crossword puzzle. The puzzle's clues are based on the *New International Version* of the Bible, but your students probably have an assortment of Bible versions. Therefore, it's a good idea to talk to each pair of students as they work, offering help and suggestions.

After students complete work, regain their attention. Go over the answer to each clue as you read Ephesians 1:1-14. Remember that some of the concepts dealt with may seem confusing to your students. You may guide them through understanding the spiritual blessings that God provides by discussing the following list of important concepts. (See also INSIGHTS FOR THE LEADER.) Begin by pointing out that these blessings are for God's people, not for everyone—

though anyone can become God's child by coming to Christ.

- Blessing—God's kindness to us.
- In Him—The spiritual union only Christians have with Jesus.
- Predestine—To decree beforehand.
- Grace—God's undeserved favor.
- Redemption—To free from captivity by paying a price.
- Mystery of His will—According to Ephesians 1:10, the fact that all things will be under Christ's rule.
- Marked with a seal—God's Spirit in us is the evidence and guarantee that we are in God's family.
- Inheritance—All the riches God gives to His adopted children.

Step 2 (10-12 minutes): Allow the students to remain in their pairs to work on this assignment. Tell them, **I want you to turn your crossword puzzle over and draw a line down the center of the paper, from top to bottom. On the left side of the line write, "God's Blessing for Us." On the right side write "Why It's Special." Now take a few minutes to list, in the left column, all the blessings you see in Ephesians 1:1-14. I also want you to add any other blessings you can think of, such as physical health or good friendships. Use the right column to explain why you may be grateful to God for each blessing.**

After allowing time for students to write, regain their attention and ask them to share examples of what they have written. If they need help listing blessings not given in Ephesians, suggest some simple things such as a home, food, clothing, family and so on. God's blessings are both spiritual and material (see Matthew 6:25-34).

Step 3 (10-13 minutes): Say, **We are going to create a graffiti poster. I want each of you to think of a word or phrase that describes a blessing you have received.** Encourage your learners to be creative. (You may motivate students by making this a contest; the people who write the three most clever statements receive prizes.)

Have students to gather around the paper you've attached to the wall. Give them marking pens and tell them to write large so that everyone can easily read what they have to say about God's wonderful blessings. If some of the students like to draw, let them add cartoons to the poster.

When the poster is complete, say something like this: **You have created a masterpiece! I hope this helps you understand some of the wonderful things that God has freely given to us who are Christians. Many people have been given much by God, but not everyone acknowledges what He has done for him or her. Let's think of a practical way to give thanks to God for what He has done for us.**

Conclusion and Decision

CONCLUSION (5-7 minutes)

Lead (or invite someone else to lead) your students in a song of praise and thanksgiving for the many blessings that your students have expressed. Select a praise song or chorus that is easy to sing and is familiar to your students.

If your students do not enjoy singing you may wish to read the words of the song as a solo while students bow their heads and consider the song as a prayer.

Close the session in prayer and distribute the Fun Page take-home paper.

The Blessings Crossword

"Praise be to the God and Father of our Lord Jesus Christ, who has blessed us in the heavenly realms with every spiritual blessing in Christ." Ephesian 1:3

You can learn about some of the great blessings God has given us by completing this crossword puzzle. It is based on Ephesians 1:1-14, which you'll need to read as you play. Each clue contains the verse where you can find the answer.

ACROSS

3. Jesus shed this for us (verse 7).
5. These have been forgiven (verse 7).
6. Paul and the Ephesians were among the first to do this (verse 12).
8. God blesses us with this for our sins (verse 7).
9. God chose us to be this in His eyes (verse 4).
10. God lavishes wisdom on us. A person with wisdom is this (verse 8).
13. We are holy and blameless in God's what? (Verse 4.)
17. God chose us before the creation of this (verse 4).
18. God did this with His grace for us (verse 8).
20. This word means that God bought us and set us free (verse 7).
21. God predestined us because of this (verse 4).
22. God has freely given us this (verse 6).
24. One of the ones in Ephesus (verse 1).
25. The gospel is the Word of what? (Verse 13.)
26. This word means that the Holy Spirit is like a down payment (verse 14).
27. We are adopted by God as these (verse 5).
28. The Holy Spirit is doing this regarding our inheritance (verse 14).

11. All things will be subjected to Christ when the times have reached this (verse 10).
12. Grace has been freely what to us? (Verse 6.)
14. Grace has been given to us in what manner? (Verse 6.)
15. We've been predestined to be this (verse 5).
16. All things on earth and where else will be under Christ? (Verse 10.)
19. The gospel is our what? (Verse 13.)
20. God's grace has lots of this (verse 7).
23. All these blessings are found in whom? (Verse 3.)

DOWN

1. This has been guaranteed by the Holy Spirit (verse 14).
2. In Him we have been this (verse 11).
3. When we were chosen in relation to the creation of the world (verse 4).
4. God is His Father (verse 3).
5. The Holy Spirit is this to us (verse 13).
7. God made the mystery what to us?(Verse 9.)
9. God has given us every spiritual one (verse 3).

TOWN CRIER

"GOD HAS BLESSED US WITH EVERY SPIRITUAL BLESSING," CLAIMS THE APOSTLE PAUL!

"Praise be to the God and Father of our Lord Jesus Christ, who has blessed us in the heavenly realms with every spiritual blessing in Christ." Ephesians 1:3

Based on Ephesians 1:1-14

Ephesus—In a letter received at the local church fellowship today, Paul the apostle claims that God has blessed us with every spiritual blessing in Christ Jesus!

Paul tells us that these blessings include:

1. God chose us before the world was even created to be holy and blameless;
2. God has planned for us to be His adopted children;
3. We have redemption in Him;
4. We have forgiveness for sins in Him.

THE **MANAGING EDITOR** OF THE **TOWN CRIER**, REPORTERS **TYPO** AND **PIFONT**, AND THEIR MASCOT, THE **NEWS HOUND**:

THINK OF IT, GUYS: GOD HAS GIVEN US ALL THESE **FANTASTIC BLESSINGS**, FREE OF CHARGE!

MY FAVORITE IS THE FACT THAT GOD HAS ADOPTED US. THINK OF ALL THE **WONDERFUL PRIVILEGES AND HONORS** THAT AWAIT US IN HEAVEN!

BE SURE TO TAKE THE **DOG** WHEN YOU GO!

WHAT'S THE MATTER, TYPO?

SOMETIMES I JUST DON'T **FEEL** BLESSED. I DON'T HAVE MUCH MONEY...I DON'T HAVE A NICE CAR...MY HOUSE IS ALL RUN DOWN...

THOSE THINGS COME AND GO, BUDDY. KEEP YOUR EYES ON ALL THE **GOOD THINGS** GOD HAS GIVEN YOU. SEE WHAT I MEAN?

YEAH, I SEE WHAT YOU MEAN.

THERE ARE TWO KINDS OF BLESSINGS. THERE ARE TEMPORARY BLESSINGS LIKE GOOD HEALTH, MONEY, A SCHOOL HOLIDAY. THESE THINGS ARE NICE BLESSINGS, BUT THEY COME AND GO. THEN THERE ARE PERMANENT BLESSINGS, LIKE FORGIVENESS OF SINS, ETERNAL LIFE, THE RICHES OF HEAVEN AND SO ON. IF YOU ARE A CHRISTIAN, THESE BLESSINGS ARE YOURS! GOD HAS PROMISED THEM TO THOSE WHO LOVE HIM AND FOLLOW JESUS.

DON'T BE LIKE TYPO, WHO SOMETIMES HAS TROUBLE REMEMBERING HOW MUCH GOD HAS BLESSED HIM. BE LIKE PIFONT, WHO TAKES GREAT PLEASURE IN REALIZING HOW MUCH GOD LOVES US ALL!

SHOWERS OF BLESSINGS!

Instructions: Using a pencil—not a pen—draw a trail from the "Start" to the "Finish." Along the way, try to pick up as many "blessings" as you can. But you cannot **cross your own trail or use the same pipe or connector twice, not even for a fraction of an inch.** Temporary blessings, such as health or money, count five points each. Permanent blessings count ten points. The object, therefore, is to find the path with the most points. Compare your score with the chart below.

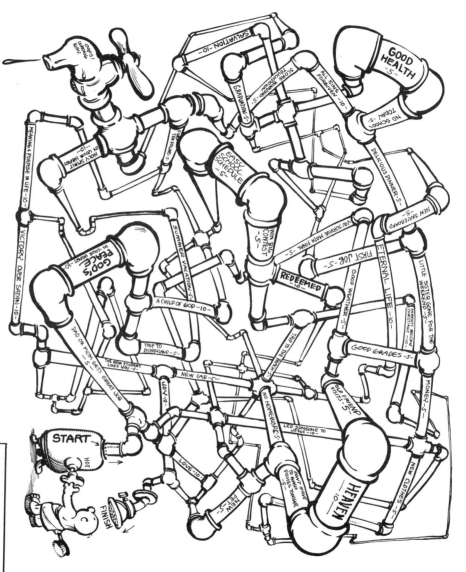

Score Chart
(Count your Blessings)

135—Lousy, try again.
150—Not bad for a first try.
175—You can do better.
195—This is the highest score we got. Can you top it?

DAILY THINKERS

Day 1 Read Ephesians 1:1. Who chose Paul to be an apostle, according to this verse? Have you ever felt God had a special assignment for you?

Day 2 Ephesians 1:3. List the spiritual blessings God has given to you. (Example: My sins are forgiven.)

Day 3 Ephesians 1:4-8. What two words describe how God wants us to appear in His sight? (See verse 4.) Underline the words which tell what we have when God adopts us.

Day 4 Ephesians 1:9,10. God has planned one head for all things in heaven and on earth. Who is He? When will He take over?

Day 5 Ephesians 1:11,12. These verses tell us God works out everything according to His will. How can you know His will? (One hint is found in 2 Timothy 3:16.)

Day 6 Ephesians 1:13,14. In these verses Paul calls the gospel of salvation "the word of truth." What is salvation? What must you do to be saved? If you do not know, ask a Christian.

THEME: Who is blessed?

Session 1

BIBLE STUDY OUTLINE

The following notes provide a skeleton upon which you can base a short Bible talk. Read Matthew 5:1-12 to your students. Make the following remarks as time allows.

Introductory remarks: God has given this world many wonderful blessings. He has provided everything people need to live and flourish. Over and above these basic natural blessings, God has reserved special blessings for those people who please Him. In His famous Sermon on the Mount, Jesus gave a list of blessings and how a person receives them.

Verses 1,2: Jesus was very popular at this time—later, the multitudes would call for His death. The crowds were attracted to Jesus at this point because of the miracles He performed and the power of His teaching. When Jesus made it clear that they must stop living for their own selfish desires and commit themselves completely to Him and His Father, most of the people fell away (see John 6:60-66). Even today there are crowds who "hang around" Jesus. There may be people in our youth group who enjoy the activities and Bible studies, but they won't last when they realize that God wants them to live pure, Christian lives.

Verse 3: The primary meaning for "blessed" is "happy." But the word has the deeper meaning of spiritual contentment and well-being. To be "poor in spirit" means to be totally dependent upon God the Father rather than on self or any other thing. A person committed to God receives eternal life in God's kingdom.

Verse 4: Even Christians face times of mourning and pain. But Jesus promises that eventually the tears of those who have committed themselves to Him will be dried and everything will be set right. Revelation 7:17 tells us that "God will wipe away every tear from their eyes." That will be an amazing experience!

Verse 5: To be meek doesn't mean to be weak and wimpy. In fact, this meekness is directed toward God. That is, we are to humble ourselves before God. When we do, we become a part of the family of God, those who inherit the future world.

Verse 6: To "hunger and thirst for righteousness" means to desire to be close to Jesus and God the Father, and to desire to do what is pleasing to God. The intensity of this hunger can be compared to a starving person's desire to be close to food. Our modern age of self-centeredness has made this attitude of wanting to please God rare. God promises to satisfy those who hunger for closeness to him.

Verse 7: To be merciful means to let someone off the hook. For example, if we don't strike back at someone who says something mean about us, God

will remember that attitude and treat us the same way. Matthew 7:2 says, "In the same way you judge others, you will be judged, and with the measure you use, it will be measured to you." Remember that God will treat you the way you treat others.

Verse 8: To be "pure in heart" is not easy. This, as well as all the other things Jesus mentions in this passage, is something no ordinary human can do on his or her own. Only the power of God can transform a sinner into someone who is pure enough to see God. Ephesians 2:4,5 says, "But because of his great love for us, God, who is rich in mercy, made us alive with Christ even when we were dead in transgressions."

Verse 9: What is a junior high peacemaker? Not only a person who stops fights, but one who helps others find the inner peace that Jesus gives. You can help a person find Jesus by doing something as simple as inviting a friend to one of our group's meetings. When you bring the message of peace to others, they will recognize that you are God's child.

Verses 10-12: Don't think that just because you are richly blessed spiritually that you will not have problems in this world. Jesus makes it clear that being identified with Him will cause us to face the same problems the prophets before us faced. But our reward will be great! We will be citizens of heaven. (Now do the Object Lesson.)

OBJECT LESSON: ALARM CLOCK

Show your listeners an alarm clock. Ask them what an alarm clock is for (to alert us to important moments). Say something like this: **Jesus has given us a list of blessings that we will receive if, with His help, we live as He tells us to. This clock reminds us that some day the world's time will run out. The alarm will go off and the world as we know it will end. Those of us who have obeyed Jesus' words will be rewarded. Those who ignore Him will be greatly—pardon the pun—alarmed.**

DISCUSSION QUESTIONS

1. **We mentioned that Jesus was popular at the time He gave the Sermon on the Mount. What things are there about Jesus that would make a junior higher like Him today?**

2. **It's a good idea to think about the blessings that God gives. Even things that don't seem like real blessings can be. School, for instance, can be boring and hard. But what are some of the blessings God can bring because of our experiences at school? What are some blessings we may receive from our jobs or at home?**

3. **What are some ways a person your age can be a blessing to others?**

A Great Way to Grow a Youth Group: the Slave Contest!

Slave contests are a wonderful means of increasing youth group attendance and encouraging kids to bring and use their Bibles! This and the next five Games and Things feature rules, tips, suggestions, games and everything else you need to know to plan and conduct a successful slave contest. Here, in simple terms, is how it all works.

The guys are "pitted" against the girls. Each person earns "slave bucks" for doing various chores that you've set up. One of the following Games and Things (Session 3) has slave bucks which you can print on a photocopier. The Games and Things for Session 5 features a list of things contestants can do to earn those bucks. A person would receive ten slave bucks, for example, by coming to Bible study. Fifty bucks would be given to a person who brought a newcomer; the newcomer would also receive fifty slave bucks. Girls get pink bucks, guys get blue.

Meanwhile, the teams are earning points (the points are entirely separate from the bucks—bucks are earned by individuals; points are earned by teams). The girls might earn a thousand points at the midweek games night, say, for having more girls in attendance than the guys. A running total of points is kept from meeting to meeting on a poster for all to see. The team with the most points one week before the official slave party wins the contest. The members of the team that wins the contest become the masters, the members of the other team have to be the slaves.

Once the winning team has been determined, the bucks held by the losing team become valueless and can be thrown away. The bucks held by the winning team are used to bid for slaves at the beginning of the slave party (see the Games and Things for Session 6).

A "slave contract" must be devised by the teams when the contest begins. The contract describes in detail the exact behavior that the slaves must exhibit at the slave party. The guys design a contract that the girls must follow if the girls become slaves, the girls devise one for the guys. You'll find a sample contract in the Games and Things for Session 2. Devote one meeting to creating the contracts. The first draft of each contract is given to the opposing team to ratify. It's up to that team and you to be sure no unreasonable requests are made on the contract. Once the boys and girls are agreed to the content of the contracts, each person who wishes to be involved in the contest must sign that person's solemn commitment to attend the slave party and abide by the contract even if he or she has to be a slave. Be sure to stress that anyone who signs the contract MUST attend the party, win or lose. A person who does not sign up cannot attend the party, but they CAN be included in a team's efforts to earn points. For instance, the team with the most in attendance at a particular meeting would win the attendance points even if some of them had not signed the contract. Give fifty slave bucks to anyone who signs the contract. Signatures can be added to the contracts at any time during the contest.

Read the Games and Things for Sessions 2-6 for important tips and details and a list of games to play at the slave party.

Wisdom

WHAT THE SESSION IS ABOUT

Through Christ we can live wisely.

SCRIPTURE STUDIED

Proverbs 3:5,6; Matthew 6:22,23; John 8:32; Ephesians 1:15-23; 5:15; James 1:5

KEY PASSAGE

"I keep asking that the God of our Lord Jesus Christ, the glorious Father, may give you the Spirit of wisdom and revelation, so that you may know him better."
Ephesians 1:17

AIMS OF THE SESSION

During this session your learners will:
1. Examine Scriptures dealing with spiritual wisdom and enlightenment;
2. Discuss how God's wisdom applies to daily life;
3. Paraphrase James 1:5.

INSIGHTS FOR THE LEADER

Ephesians 1:15-23 is actually a prayer which Paul prayed for the Ephesian Christians who would read his letter. It is a beautiful prayer which skips trivialities and gets to the heart of the Ephesians' spiritual needs.

It is a good prayer for a junior high Bible study leader to pray for his or her students. When your prayers are on the level of, "God, make them shut up and sit still," this prayer can serve as an example of a caring prayer that asks God for specific blessings.

What Paul Prayed

First, Paul never stopped giving thanks for the people he had nurtured in the faith (see v. 16). He reminded his readers that he hadn't prayed once for them and then forgotten them. He kept asking that God would give them the wisdom they needed to live as His people (see v. 17). We can learn from Paul that loving and effective prayer for junior highers means continuing, conscious practice.

Second, Paul asked that God would give the people "the Spirit of wisdom and revelation, so that you may know him better" (v. 17). Paul did not pray that the Ephesians would know a lot of memorized facts, but that they would know God. Knowing facts is fine, but knowing God is of first importance. "The fear of the Lord is the beginning of wisdom, and knowledge of the Holy One is understanding" (Proverbs 9:10). The end result of this

wisdom is to better know the Lord, which will result in being set free (see John 8:32) to grow and develop in areas that we had never thought possible. It's possible for junior highers to learn all the facts about Jesus and still not know Him. As their teacher, you can help them by continually showing that Jesus is a person who can be known here and now. Your loving them with His love will take them a big step beyond "just the facts."

In Ephesians 1:18 Paul used a phrase that is reminiscent of Christ's teaching in Matthew 6:22,23: "The eye is the lamp of the body. If your eyes are good, your whole body will be full of light. But if your eyes are bad, your whole body will be full of darkness. If then the light within you is darkness, how great is that darkness!" Jesus was clearly teaching about the same kind of inner enlightenment to which Paul was referring.

It is interesting to consider that even Christians need enlightenment and wisdom. Arrival at a saving trust in Christ is not the end of the journey, but the beginning. Paul realized that there is still much about the Christian life that believers need to see and understand.

Paul went on to pray that as a result of knowing God, the Ephesians would know three other things:

"The hope to which he has called you" (Ephesians 1:18). Knowing the Lord gives us hope for His help in this life, and hope for

NOTES

heaven with Him. The definition of "hope" in the Bible is something very different from our common interpretation of the word. Paul was not using the word to mean "wish." Instead, "hope" in the Scriptures means a confident expectation. Our hope in God is sure because He is sure. To your junior highers, hope may be a far-off abstraction, because it has to do with the future while they live in the present. But hope can become meaningful to them; hope tells them that when they fail, God picks them up again and again and gives them another chance.

"The riches of his glorious inheritance in the saints" (v. 18). The "saints" are all Christians, those who have received Him and the redemption He provides. Our "inheritance" is what we receive as children of God. In Session 1 you looked at Paul's catalog of the benefits we receive in Christ—the knowledge that we are chosen by God and that He sees us as holy and blameless; the privilege of being adopted into His family; the forgiveness of sin. Paul prayed that the Ephesians would come to fully understand those benefits. You can be glad when your junior highers grasp any of those benefits in a more complete way; in this life no one will fully understand and appreciate them, but we can grow in our understanding.

"His incomparably great power for us who believe" (v. 19) describes the rest of Paul's prayer (which is also the rest of the Scripture for this session). It is about God's power in us, the same power that raised Christ from the dead. At first your junior highers may be attracted to Christ's power as if it is something they can use to get what they want or to make things turn out as they wish. (Many adults are tempted the same way!)

God's Power

God does not offer us His power to use for our own ambitions. He is strong on our behalf, working out what is good for us, but we are in submission to His power, not in control: "God placed all things under his feet and appointed him to be head over everything for the church" (v. 22). Because He is all-powerful, nothing can snatch us out of His care, nothing can hurt us without His permission and no temptation has final say over us. Your junior highers may feel incapable and stumbling in many areas of life; but God is at work for them. They can be comforted knowing that their ability to cope in life is up to the power of God, not up to their uncertain skills.

A final note on wisdom and knowledge: In the Bible, "knowledge" usually has to do with the perception of truth, while "wisdom" is the practical application of truth to real-life situations. In this session your learners will find out that they can know God's truth and they will think of wise ways to apply their knowledge.

SESSION PLAN

BEFORE CLASS BEGINS: The first two Teaching Resource pages comprise a game called "The Wisdom Walk." Read the instructions on "The Wisdom Walk" for materials for spinner. Photocopy both pages (enlarge them if your copier is able) and tape each set together to form a game board. Make one game board for every three or four students. Provide some sort of game token for each player, such as a washer, peanut or bit of colored paper. Photocopy the Fun Page (which is used in the ATTENTION GRABBER). There is no Key worksheet this time. The third Teaching Resource page does not need to be photocopied. See the second step of the EXPLORATION for special instructions and materials.

Attention Grabber

ATTENTION GRABBER (5-7 minutes)

Tell your students, **Today's subject from Ephesians is wisdom. This is game playing day; we have three different games we are going to try. The first one is a simple one from the Fun Page. It's really more of a fun do-it-yourself wisdom test than a game.**

Give your learners a few minutes to work "The Wisdom Rate-O-Mometer" game on the Fun Page. The game is a combination of tongue-in-cheek humor and profound truths from the Bible. Quickly discuss each question and ask the class to indicate how well they fared on the ratings.

Say something like this: **Well, you did better in the ratings than I thought! Maybe you're a bit wiser than the average junior high class. As I said, wisdom is today's topic, so let's play another game, one based on some important wisdom from God's Word.**

Bible Exploration

EXPLORATION (30-40 minutes)

Step 1 (15-20 minutes): Distribute "The Wisdom Walk" games and the playing tokens. Direct students in forming groups of three or four. Go over the rules printed on the board, then let them play.

Call time before any group has completed a game. (This happens when all spaces are initialed by

every player. In such a case there would be no winner as all players would have the maximum number of points.)

Review with your students the answers to the game questions. Add any appropriate comments from your own study in Ephesians or from the materials in the INSIGHTS FOR THE LEADER. Point out that: godly wisdom will help a Christian know God better; that knowledge of God's truth leads to freedom of the "inside" person no matter what his or her outer circumstances may be; that knowing God gives light in a dark world and that trusting the Lord opens the Christian to receiving His help in daily life.

Step 2 (15-20 minutes): This final game will help students apply "The Wisdom Walk" game's Scripture truths to real life situations. Before class, tape several Styrofoam cups together as shown in the illustration (or use heavy mugs). Cut apart the questions and situations on the third Teaching Resource page and place them randomly in most of the cups (two or more can go in one cup). In the remaining cups, place candy bars and other small rewards. To play the game you need a coin, peanut or other marker that the players can toss into the cups.

When ready to play, place the cups on the floor 8-10 feet from a tape line behind which students will stand. Explain, **We are going to play a game of skill. I've filled the cups with questions and rewards. I'll give each of you at least one chance to stand behind the line and toss this peanut in a cup. If you get a cup with a candy bar, it's yours. If you get a cup with questions in it, I will draw out one question, read it and let you answer it.**

Have students line up behind the line and toss the marker. You can discard each question as it is answered. The questions are rather thought-provoking, so it's a good idea to allow the entire class to help answer each one. Be sure to add any needed insights and to congratulate each student for his or her efforts.

Conclusion and Decision

CONCLUSION (5-7 minutes)

Say, **We've been talking about practical wisdom for daily life. Where does this sort of wisdom come from? James 1:5 says, "If any of you lacks wisdom, he should ask God, who gives generously to all without finding fault, and it will be given to him." If you need wisdom to do the right thing, the best place to go is to the Lord.**

Instruct students to read James 1:5 from their Bibles and to paraphrase it in fifteen words or less on a sheet of scratch paper. Collect the papers to review students' efforts after class.

Close with audible prayer, asking specifically that your students will be enlightened to make the choices God wants them to make.

Distribute the Fun Page take-home paper.

The WISDOM WALK

This game is based on Proverbs 3:5,6; Matthew 6:22,23; John 8:32; Ephesians 1:17-19,22,23 and Ephesians 5:15. These are the passages you'll need to look up as you play the game. Use your Bible's table of contents if necessary.

STUFF YOU NEED: A Bible, a playing piece for each player (bottle cap, coin or used tonsil), a paper clip and pencil.

TO PLAY: Players spin the paper clip on the spinner (see illustration) to see who goes first. The player who spins the highest number is first. Players spin to see how many spaces to jump their tokens. Two playing tokens may not occupy the same space; players must remain where they are if there is no unoccupied space to which they may move. Most spaces have questions on them—the first time a player lands on such a space he or she must answer the question there. When the question is answered correctly (you can use your Bible), that player is awarded the number of points on the space and writes his or her initials on the space. Other spaces have silly things that a player may do (if desired) to earn points. A player may score points and write his or her initials only once for each space; a space may be initialed by each player. Players keep going around the board until time is called. Add the total points when the game is over. Player with the highest score wins.

ONE POINT IF YOU CAN IMITATE PEE WEE HERMAN.

HOW ARE WE TO BEHAVE, ACCORDING TO EPHESIANS 5:15? THREE POINTS.

READ EPHESIANS 1:19. WHAT IS THE GREAT THING WE CAN HAVE? THREE POINTS.

WHAT IS CHRIST THE HEAD OF, ACCORDING TO EPHESIANS 1:22,23? TWO POINTS.

BONUS FIVE POINTS THE FIRST TIME YOU LAND HERE.

THREE POINTS IF YOU CROW LIKE A ROOSTER.

TWO POINTS IF YOU CAN MAKE ANY OF YOUR FINGERS GO "DOUBLE-JOINTED."

WHAT DID PAUL PRAY FOR IN EPHESIANS 1:18? TWO POINTS.

THREE POINTS IF YOU CAN SAY YOUR NAME WITH A DONALD DUCK VOICE.

START

Place the pencil like this and spin the paper clip with your finger.

BONUS THREE POINTS THE FIRST TIME YOU LAND HERE.

WHAT BIBLE PASSAGE INDICATES THAT PEOPLE CAN HAVE SPIRITUAL DARKNESS INSIDE THEM? FOUR POINTS

FOUR POINTS IF YOU CAN HOLD YOUR TOES FIRMLY IN YOUR HANDS AND JUMP THE WIDTH OF YOUR BIBLE.

WHAT DID GOD PLACE UNDER JESUS' FEET, ACCORDING TO EPHESIANS 1:22? THREE POINTS.

WHAT PASSAGE SAYS THAT GOD WILL STRAIGHTEN OUT YOUR PATHS IF YOU TRUST IN HIM? THREE POINTS.

WHAT DID PAUL PRAY FOR IN EPHESIANS 1:17? TWO POINTS.

WHY DID PAUL WANT HIS READERS TO HAVE THE SPIRIT OF WISDOM AND REVELATION (SEE EPHESIANS 1:17)? TWO POINTS.

BONUS FOUR POINTS THE FIRST TIME YOU LAND HERE.

TWO POINTS IF YOU CAN ROLL YOUR TONGUE. FIVE POINTS IF YOU CAN ROLL IT UPSIDE DOWN (THE TONGUE, NOT YOU)!

WHAT BIBLE PASSAGE TELLS US THAT IF WE FOLLOW CHRIST'S TEACHING, HIS TRUTH WILL SET US FREE? THREE POINTS.

Cut apart all these situations and questions as instructed in the second step of the EXPLORATION.

John 8:32 says that Christ's truth can set us free. That means we can be trapped by sin. Let's say our youth group has fallen into the trap of little cliques—small groups of kids who exclude and ignore the other kids. You don't like it. What could you do to help free the youth group from the trap of cliques?	Proverbs 3:6 says to acknowledge God in all your ways. A friend who is a Mormon is putting a lot of pressure on you to attend his youth group. Name one way you could acknowledge God in this instance.	You are collecting money on your paper route. One of your customers claims that he does not owe you money. You know that he does. What would be the wise thing to do or say?
Matthew 6:22,23 indicates that people can be filled with spiritual darkness. How can a person become filled with God's wisdom—spiritual light?	You buy some stereo equipment from a kid at school. Then you hear from some other kids that the equipment was stolen! What would be the wise thing to do or say?	You and your parents are having a conflict over your clothes and hairstyle. What would be the wise thing to do, say or think?
You find a valuable ring in the street. What would be the wise thing to do with it?	You lost your father's valuable silver pen at school. What would be the wise thing to do?	You have a weekend job (and it's hard for a kid your age to find a job). The problem is, they want you to work during the time you usually go to the worship service. What would be the wise thing to do?
It's time for "The Big Test" in History. You haven't studied as well as you should have. What would be the wise thing to do?	While on a camping trip, your friends try to get you to push yourself to your limits by daring you to climb up a dangerous cliff. What should you do or say?	Your brother accidentally wrecked your priceless comic book collection. (He dropped a fishbowl on it. The fish was in bad shape, too!) What should you do or say?
Your best friend is lying to her mom—using you as an alibi. (She said she was at your house when she was really out with her boyfriend.) What would be the wise thing to do about this situation?	You have to go to Aunt Mildred's house this weekend. You are not very happy about it—there are a million and one things that you would rather do! What would be the wise attitude to assume?	You have some questions about the origin of the Bible and the reliability of Scripture. Where would be a wise place to find answers to your questions?
Some people you know are inviting you to get "loaded" with them. What would be the wise thing to do? Why?	After your friend leaves your house you notice that a piece of your clothing is missing. What would be a wise thing to do or say?	Some of your friends are putting down others in your youth group. What would be the wise thing to do or say?
	A friend comes to you and says that he or she is not happy with his or her life. What would be a wise thing to do or say?	Your best friend's favorite grandma has died suddenly. What would be the wise thing to do or say?

TOWN CRIER

Front Page

NUTTY PROFESSOR CONDUCTS HAIR-RAISING EXPERIMENT!

"Boy, this really burns me up," said Square.

THE WISDOM RATE-O-MOMETER

Instructions: Starting at the bottom with question #1, answer each question yes or no. Here's how to do it: Use a pencil or pen to follow the path of arrows that your answers to each question lead you on. When you reach the top, your "Wisdom Rating" will tell you just how wise—or not—you are. Some of the questions are serious, some are tongue-in-cheek.

WISDOM RATING:

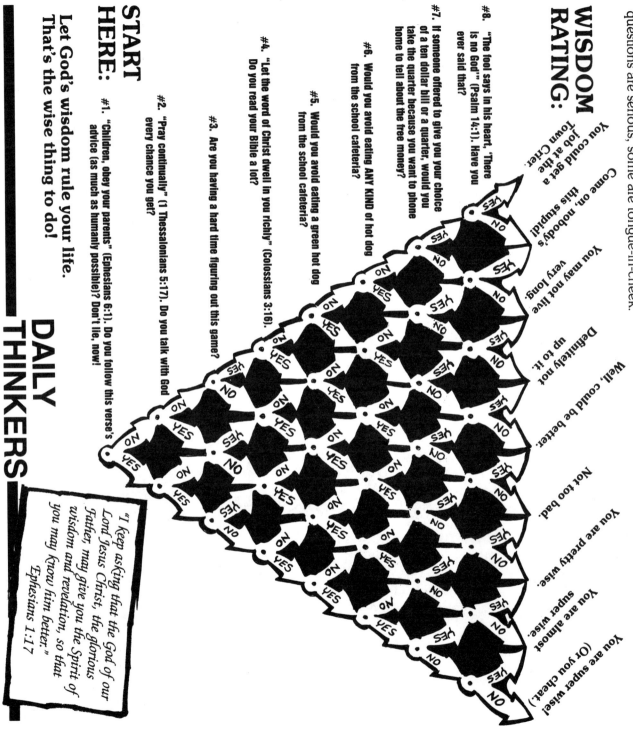

You could get a job at the Town Crier.

Come on, nobody's this stupid!

You may not live very long.

Definitely not up to it.

Well, could be better.

Not too bad.

You are pretty wise.

You are almost super wise.

You are super wise! (Or you cheat!)

#8. "The fool says in his heart, 'There is no God'" (Psalm 14:1). Have you ever said that?

#7. If someone offered to give you your choice of a ten dollar bill or a quarter, would you take the quarter because you want to phone home to tell about the free money?

#6. Would you avoid eating ANY KIND of hot dog from the school cafeteria?

#5. Would you avoid eating a green hot dog from the school cafeteria?

#4. "Let the word of Christ dwell in you richly" (Colossians 3:16). Do you read your Bible a lot?

#3. Are you having a hard time figuring out this game?

#2. "Pray continually" (1 Thessalonians 5:17). Do you talk with God every chance you get?

START HERE:

#1. "Children, obey your parents" (Ephesians 6:1). Do you follow this verse's advice (as much as humanly possible)? Don't lie, now!

Let God's wisdom rule your life. That's the wise thing to do!

DAILY THINKERS

Day 1 Read Ephesians 1:15,16. What caused Paul to give thanks for the Christians at Ephesus? Would Paul be able to give thanks for you?

Day 2 Ephesians 1:17. What help does God give so you may better understand Him? What does revelation mean?

Day 3 Ephesians 1:18. Why do you think Paul wanted these Christians to understand with the "eyes of their hearts"? Does this also apply to Christians today?

Day 4 Ephesians 1:19,20. What example does Paul give of God's great power? Can you give another example of God's power?

Day 5 Ephesians 1:21. According to this Scripture one ruler is above all in this present age and in the age to come. Who is He? (See verse 20.) What kind of power and authority does He have?

Day 6 Ephesians 1:22,23. Who is the head of the Church? Where is He? What is the Church? Where is it now? Draw a picture of the Church using these verses as a guide.

"I keep asking that the God of our Lord Jesus Christ, the glorious Father, may give you the Spirit of wisdom and revelation, so that you may know him better."
Ephesians 1:17

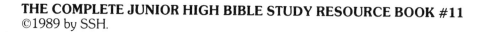

THEME: Living wisely.

Session 2

BIBLE STUDY OUTLINE

Read Proverbs 1:1; 2:1-9 to your students. (You might wish to expand your message with additional verses in Proverbs.) Make the following remarks as time allows.

Introductory remarks: Have you ever opened a soda can just after someone vigorously shook it? Have you ever tried to look at your watch while holding a full chocolate shake—dumping it into your lap? How did you feel? Like a fool! We all have times when we feel very stupid. But how many of us have times when we feel very wise? It seems as though stupidity comes naturally, but wisdom has to be acquired and developed.

If you want to be a wise person, then you'll want to get in the habit of reading the Bible every day. It contains God's wisdom to live by. The book of Proverbs is an excellent place to find lots of wisdom in short, easy-to-read passages.

Proverbs 1:1: Solomon was reputed to be the wisest man on earth. First Kings 3 contains the story of how he came to be so wise. God appeared to Solomon in a dream and offered to give him anything he wanted. As the king of Israel, Solomon asked God to give him a discerning heart to govern God's people and to distinguish between right and wrong. God was very pleased at Solomon's request and gave him riches and honor as well as great wisdom. Solomon wrote thousands of proverbs—distilled bits of practical wisdom—and several hundred of these are preserved in the book of Proverbs.

Proverbs 2:1: What is wisdom? It is living the best possible life as God intended it to be lived. How do we get this wisdom? Solomon tells us how. First, accept God's words and commands (Solomons' words and commands have their source in God). To accept means to follow and obey—not just to agree with them without responding to them.

Verse 2: You have ears—listen carefully for wisdom. When you hear it, set it in the center of your being, your heart.

Verse 3: You have a mouth—use it to ask for wisdom. You can ask God in prayer for wisdom and you can ask the advice of wise people around you.

Verse 4: You have eyes—recognize the value of wisdom and

search for it as diligently as a prospector looks for gold.

Verses 5,6: You have a brain—let God fill it up with wisdom. To fear God is to lovingly obey Him and submit to Him as Lord and King. When we enter into that sort of relationship with God, we can truly begin to have wisdom and to know Him with all the privileges and pleasures that brings.

Verses 7,8: What do we get when we live wisely in submission to God? We get victory and a shield of protection. Remember that the next time you are worried about the future or circumstances around you.

Verse 9: One of the great things about being filled with God's wisdom is that God will guide you along the proper path in life. People without God have to slog through this complex world on their own, but you can have God's map in your hands. (Now do the Object Lesson.)

OBJECT LESSON: SPONGE

Dip a large sponge into a bowl of water, allowing the sponge to be saturated. Say something like this: **For its size, a sponge can soak up an amazing amount of water. You can soak up God's wisdom like a sponge. If you saturate yourself with God's Word, you will find that God will bless you with an exciting, rewarding life.**

DISCUSSION QUESTIONS

1. **It's usually pretty easy to tell the difference between a wise person and a fool. What are some of the telltale signs of wisdom and foolishness in a person?**

2. **We said that it seems as though stupidity comes naturally, but wisdom has to be acquired and developed. Why do you suppose wisdom is so rare?**

3. **First Corinthians 1:30 tells us that "Jesus . . . has become for us wisdom from God." If Jesus is God's wisdom for us, how do we tap into that wisdom?**

Slave Contract

Here is a sample "slave contract" that suggests the sort of contracts the girls and guys should devise for your youth group's slave contest. This sample contract was written by the guys' team; the girls would have to abide by the stipulations on this contract if they lost the contest and thus were the slaves at the slave party. Notice that this contract requires the girls to each provide up to three dollars worth of food for the party. You may wish to lower this amount or eliminate it altogether by providing the refreshments yourself.

When your guys and girls have written and ratified their two contracts (see the previous Games and Things for details), glue each to a large sheet of poster board. The poster board will give everyone space to write his/her names, phone numbers, addresses and signatures. Write "Girls' Contract" and "Guys' Contract" at the top of the appropriate posters. Be sure to provide an opportunity for newcomers to sign the contracts at each meeting until just before the winning team is determined.

GIRLS' CONTRACT

ATTIRE: Slaves must wear tattered rags to the party and be barefoot.

FOOD: A slave must bring one slice of pizza, a cup full of grapes, two candy bars and two colas. Slaves are not required to spend more than three dollars.

SLAVES MUST ALSO PROVIDE: Two cushions or pillows and a soft blanket for their master's comfort. They must also bring a fan—hand or electric. A kazoo or other musical instrument and one funny joke must also be provided.

MANNER OF ADDRESS: Slaves will address their masters as "O Grand One, I bow before thee" or "Yes, O Party Master."

EXPECTED BEHAVIOR: Slaves must peel and serve grapes. Slaves must run all errands for refreshments. Slaves must fan their masters. They must perform in any of the party's games and contests. Slaves must bow on their knees when addressing their masters. Slaves must clean up any mess. Slaves must have one funny joke to tell to everyone.

PUNISHMENT: Slaves who will not obey a command must appear before the party's judge for trial and punishment. Punishment must be approved by the judge.

Alive in Christ
SESSION 3

WHAT THE SESSION IS ABOUT

Christ has saved us from death in sin to life in Himself.

SCRIPTURE STUDIED

Ephesians 2:1-5

KEY PASSAGE

"But because of his great love for us, God, who is rich in mercy, made us alive with Christ even when we were dead in transgressions—it is by grace you have been saved."
Ephesians 2:4,5

AIMS OF THE SESSION

During this session your learners will:

1. Examine biblical teaching about being dead in sin versus being alive in Christ;
2. Discuss contemporary ways in which sin and Christlikeness are manifested;
3. Thank God for His gift of spiritual life and tell God one way they need Him to help bring change in their lives.

INSIGHTS FOR THE LEADER

The first five verses of Ephesians 2 are packed with meaning. First Paul describes our old life, which was no life at all but actually death. (We were "dead . . . in transgressions," see vv. 1-3.) Then he exultantly writes about what God did in Jesus Christ to rescue us and make us alive (vv. 4,5).

An adult who has led a life of degrading sin and then has found life in Christ can easily identify with these verses. So can a junior high student who has recently made a firm decision to turn away from the world's pressures and follow Christ. But what about the person—junior higher or adult—who has grown up in the Christian faith and has never had to make a radical break with the past? What does this passage say to him or her?

Many of your students may be in just that position of having no "old life" to contrast with their "new life." They are in your Bible study because they always have been, not because they've found a new and exciting faith. They can't remember being "dead in transgressions" because they've never outwardly participated in the obvious sins of the world. Being a Christian, to them, seems "business as usual" rather than a vital transformation of being made alive in Christ.

Ephesians 2:1-5 does speak to young people who have grown up in the Church! How? It tells them that they need to be saved even though they have been "good kids." It tells them that God loves them and wants to show them mercy. And it tells them the difference between living for Christ and living sinfully. If they committed their lives to Christ early in life, it shows them the grief and trouble they have avoided!

Paul mentions two signs of an existence "dead in transgressions": Following the world and following selfish desires.

Following the World

"As for you, you were dead in your transgressions and sins, in which you used to live when you followed the ways of this world and the ruler of the kingdom of the air" (vv. 1,2). Your junior highers long to be accepted by their peers. You may sometimes despair over their slavish conformity to current fashion in clothing, jewelry, gimmicks, hair styles. But remember that they are doing their best to win approval from friends. Fitting in with peers is a way for young adolescents to ease themselves away from dependence on their parents; peer approval becomes a bridge to independence and maturity. The danger comes when your students get their moral values from their peers; then they are following "the ways of this world" (v. 2) in a sense that displeases God.

There are two lessons here for the junior high Sunday School teacher. First, you can reassure your students that they don't have to be different in every way in order to be Chris-

43

NOTES

tians. For example, wearing a particular brand of tennis shoes because they're popular is not a moral offense, but being sexually promiscuous is. Second, if you're going to tell your students not to follow the crowd, you must also be positive and give them a good alternative to follow: Jesus. You do want them to conform—but to Christ, not to the world!

Following Selfish Desires

"All of us also lived among them at one time, gratifying the cravings of our sinful nature and following its desires and thoughts" (v. 3). Here the pressure to sin is not from the world outside, but from our own sin nature. Maybe your students don't outwardly follow the world's questionable styles or values. That's good; but what are they following on the inside? Some may be going their own way, chasing personal ambitions—living for themselves rather than for Christ. Self-centeredness is as big a sin as worldliness; it's also much harder to spot! It's possible for a person to look like a good Christian while living for the gratification of his or her ego. You'll give your young people a spiritual boost if you help them see that being selfish is as bad for spiritual life as being worldly.

In either case, whether the junior higher struggles with external temptations of the world or internal temptations of selfish desire, the cure is the same. "It is by grace you have been saved" (v. 5). God's grace—His unearned love and mercy—is always available to the most stumbling Christian. "Let us then approach the throne of grace with confidence, so that we may receive mercy and find grace to help us in our time of need" (Hebrews 4:16).

SESSION PLAN

BEFORE CLASS BEGINS: Photocopy the Fun Page (which is used in Step 3 of the EXPLORATION). There is no Key student worksheet or Teaching Resource page this time. See the ALTERNATE ATTENTION GRABBER for special material. The CONCLUSION activity is a celebration of God's gift of spiritual life. Provide simple refreshments such as soft drinks and cookies.

Attention Grabber

ATTENTION GRABBER (3-5 minutes)

To introduce today's subject of spiritual death and spiritual life, talk about something your students can readily grasp—physical death and physical life. If you had a loved pet that died, describe your feelings about its death. Contrast the pet's activities before and after death. Obviously, the pet was not moving after death. Tell your students that in the same way, a person who is spiritually dead is unable to have any sort of involvement in God's realm, the spiritual realm. Just as a dead animal or person is unable to make itself alive, a spiritually dead person is also unable to do anything at all to come alive spiritually. Only God, who gives life, can provide a way for a person to become spiritually alive.

Say, **The Bible has some important things to say about being spiritually dead and spiritually alive. Let's take a look at this subject and how it should affect our lives.**

ALTERNATE ATTENTION GRABBER (3-5 minutes)

Bring a fresh whole chicken from the grocery store to class. When ready to begin, unwrap the chicken and show it to your students. Say something like this, **Here we've got your typical chicken. I've got a question for you: Is this chicken alive or dead?**

When students supply the obvious answer, ask them how they can be so sure. What are the telltale signs of death? Point out that the chicken was healthy and alive at one time. Contrast the natures of physical and spiritual life and death as in the original ATTENTION GRABBER. Then say, **The Bible has some important things to say about being spiritually dead and spiritually alive. Let's take a look at this subject and how it should affect our lives.**

NOTES

Bible Exploration

EXPLORATION (35-45 minutes)

Step 1 (8-10 minutes): Read Ephesians 2:1-5 aloud. Help students discuss the following questions:

1. What words does this Bible passage use to describe people who live sinfully?

2. What verse says we used to sin when we lived by the standards of the world?
   What are some ways people your age tend to follow the crowd?

3. What verse says we used to sin by being controlled by our own selfish desires?
   What are some selfish desires people your age tend to have?

4. What are the results of continuing to live controlled by the sinful nature? (See Galatians 5:19-21 for help.)

5. What did God do to help us out of this mess? (Also see Romans 5:6-9 for help.)

6. Why did God do that?

7. What are the results of what God did?

Step 2 (12-15 minutes): On the chalkboard write the following:

W = WORLD
S = SELF
C = CHRIST

Explain, **I'm going to read some case studies that could have come from typical junior high students' lives. Then we'll vote on whether the person in the case study is living for the world, for self or for Christ. Here's how you vote. Hold up three fingers to make a *W* for "world." Cross your fingers to make an *S* for "self." Make a *C* with your thumb and index finger for "Christ."**

Demonstrate the three hand signals so all learners understand how to vote. (See illustration.)

NOTES

Read the following case studies aloud. After reading each one take a vote on what it seems the person quoted is living for. If votes differ, ask students to explain; some of the case studies may fall into more than one category. For example, the boy in case study six may want a girlfriend for his own ego (self); or because having a girlfriend is the only way to be "in" at his school (world).

1. "I just got my report card and I got straight A's! Wow! Thanks, God, for making me so brilliant. Please help all those poor dummies who don't have my brains; I sure feel sorry for them."

2. "Oh boy! I got invited to Angela's party after the game! Everybody who's anybody is going to be there. Her parents are away for the weekend. I know Mom and Dad wouldn't like what goes on at Angela's parties, but I've waited a long time for this invitation and I've GOT to go!"

3. "I don't always think my parents' rules are fair. I really don't want to obey them. But I guess God knew what He was doing when He gave me these parents. I'll ask Him to help me and maybe I'll feel better about doing what they say."

4. "It's a lot of work to stay awake and read my Bible. But the more I read it, the more I see the good things God wants to do for me. So I'll keep at it."

5. "I bow my head and close my eyes when it's time to pray in worship service. Somebody might be watching me."

6. "I used to forget to bring my Bible to nearly every Bible study. But not any more! I always remember to bring it. See, there's this new girl in my Bible study, and she's always talking about the Lord. If she sees me carrying my Bible all the time, maybe she'll think I'm OK. She might even like me!"

7. "Last week I was tempted to help Jana steal something from a store. God sent Liz along at just the right minute and I remembered how neat it is to have Christian friends. Sure, I'd have liked to split the loot with Jana, but I know it's better this way."

8. "John is in the remedial reading class. The other kids make fun of him sometimes. I don't feel much like helping him, but I do it anyway. God has helped me a lot, and I guess I should help other people."

Step 3 (15-20 minutes): Distribute the Fun Page and some scratch paper and pencils. Show the students the imaginary letters on the Fun Page. Explain the scriptural background indicated by each letter and ask volunteers to read the letters aloud to the class.
Write this list on the chalkboard:

> Prisoner in jail
> Soldier on battlefield
> Astronaut in space
> Person with terminal cancer
> Person who was demon-possessed
> Any other person you can think of

Now say, **I want each of you to write a pretend letter from one of these people I've listed on the chalkboard. The letter should explain what the person was like before he or she discovered Christ, and how he or she may feel now about becoming spiritually alive. You can address the letter to the person's family or whomever you think is appropriate.**
Gather the letters and read a few of them to the class. You may display the letters on the wall.

Conclusion and Decision

CONCLUSION (8-10 minutes)

Tell students, **I want you to write one more letter, a very short one. I want you to write a letter to God. If you are a Christian, tell Him how you appreciate having His gift of spiritual life. Also write down one area in your life where you need God's help to further change and improve. If you are not a Christian, be honest with God. If you want to, tell Him that you would like to become a Christian and gain eternal life. Or admit to Him you are not interested right now. Whatever the case, your letters are private; no one will look at them. As you write, I'm going to hand out some refreshments so that we can have a little party. Our party is to celebrate the fact that God has provided a way for us to gain spiritual life.**

Before students dig in to the refreshments, lead a prayer of thanksgiving for the refreshments and for God's loving gift of life. Dismiss the class.

TOWN CRIER

JESUS RAISES LAZARUS FROM THE DEAD!   Based on John 11

By staff reporters Typo and Pifont

Bethany—The citizens of this small town were astonished today when the well-known Jesus of Nazareth raised local townsman Lazarus from the dead!

"It's a miracle," the people shouted as they ran through the dusty streets rejoicing. The mayor proclaimed a holiday, and shops and stores closed for the occasion. Camel traffic was tied up for hours.

Lazarus, still a little woozy, was asked what it was like to be dead. "I didn't even know I was," he joked. "I'm just glad I wasn't cremated, though I suppose Jesus could have fixed that, too."

Jesus was unavailable for comment, but it is reported that hundreds of people were asking Him to raise other friends and relatives buried in the local cemetery. The town's mortician, who stands to lose a lot of money on the deal, is in serious condition from a heart attack.

THE BIBLE HAS THIS TO SAY ABOUT SIN: "FOR ALL HAVE SINNED AND FALL SHORT OF THE GLORY OF GOD" (ROMANS 3:23) AND "THE WAGES OF SIN IS DEATH" (ROMANS 6:23). SINCE SIN IS DEATH, AND ALL HAVE SINNED, THAT MEANS ALL PEOPLE ARE DEAD—EVEN US "GOOD" ONES. THAT'S REALITY, NOT JUST FIGURATIVE LANGUAGE —

"YOU WERE DEAD IN YOUR TRANSGRESSIONS AND SINS" (EPHESIANS 2:1).

BUT DON'T WORRY!! IF YOU ARE A CHRISTIAN, REJOICE THAT GOD HAS MADE YOU ALIVE! READ EPHESIANS 2:4,5 —ON THE OTHER SIDE OF THE FUN PAGE.

Did you know that Christians have the wonderful privilege of being already raised from spiritual death? Now that's something worth writing home about!

In fact, here are some imaginary letters and announcements from people and acquaintances of people who were raised from physical or spiritual death or had their lives radically changed by Jesus.

From the man who became Paul the apostle, based on Acts 9:1-22.

Dear Ma:

A funny thing happened to me on the road to Damascus. You see, I was heading to Damascus to murder and persecute and jail people who believe in Jesus, known as the Christ. You know, my usual fun weekend. Suddenly, a brilliant light from heaven flashed around me! I fell down and heard a voice saying, "Saul, Saul, why do you persecute me?" It was Jesus Himself! Really, Ma. I know it sounds crazy! And guess what: I'm blind! It's not easy writing when you're blind. Anyway...

Dear Ma:

Hey, Ma! I'm cured!! I can see again! And are you ready for this? I'm a believer! Yes! I am saved! Jesus is my Lord! I'll write more about it soon.

P.S. I'm thinking of changing my name. I thought maybe Irving or Wilbur or somethin'. Got any ideas?

SAUL

A letter from Lazarus, based on John 11.

Dear Jacob:

I want to warmly thank you and your family for attending my funeral. I hope you had a good time. The flowers you brought were lovely; lilies are my favorite. You may have heard that I've been raised from the dead. Thus, the funeral was sort of a waste of time and I want to apologize for wrecking your weekend. Also, I realize that you had to buy expensive black suits for you and your kids to wear at my funeral—but hang onto them because, who knows, I may get sick and die again one of these days. I'm not making a point of it, however.

Yours truly,

Lazarus

The woman at the well, John 4:4-26.

Dear John, Eleazar, Boaz, Joseph and Barney:

I met a man named Jesus at Jacob's well while I was fetching water. He told me to go get my husband and I said I had no husband. He said I was right, because the man I was living with was not my husband and I was divorced from all of you guys before! Naturally, I perceived that Jesus was a prophet. Well, to make a long story short, I'm now a believer, a follower of Jesus. I just thought I'd write and let all you guys know, and to apologize for any inconveniences or bad feelings our past may have caused you.

Love,

Samaritan Sal

The thief on the cross, who was crucified at the side of Jesus. Based on Luke 23:39-43.

Dear Manny:

Seeing as how I've been nailed to a cross, it's difficult to write, especially with a typewriter. But something wonderful has happened that I want you to know about. Today a man named Jesus, whom I truly believe is from heaven, told me that I will be with Him in paradise this very day! Well, time is short. I gotta go. (And when you gotta go, you gotta go.)

P.S. If possible, I'll send a souvenir.

Bugsy

If you like, take a few minutes to write your own letter, explaining what your "from death to life" experience was like. If you haven't yet become a Christian or aren't sure about it, talk to your Bible teacher or a trusted Christian friend. Do it NOW!

"But because of his great love for us, God, who is rich in mercy, made us alive with Christ even when we were dead in transgressions—it is by grace you have been saved."

Ephesians 2:4,5

DAILY THINKERS

Day 1 Read Ephesians 2:1-3. Three enemies of your soul are spoken of in these verses. Can you find them? List some of the "ways of this world," which would be displeasing to God today.

Day 2 Ephesians 2:4,5. What does it mean to be saved by grace? Why did God do this for you?

Day 3 Ephesians 2:6,7. How has God shown His kindness to you through Jesus?

Day 4 Ephesians 2:8. Memorize this verse. Since salvation is God's gift to us, what can we do to receive this gift?

Day 5 Ephesians 2:9. Can salvation be bought with good works? Why not?

Day 6 Ephesians 2:10. List good works you can do at home.

THEME: How Jesus handled temptation.
Session 3

BIBLE STUDY OUTLINE

Read Matthew 4:1-11 to your students. Make the following comments as time permits.

Introductory remarks: Ephesians 2:1-5 tells us that we were all spiritually dead in our sins, following after Satan and our own evil desires. Some of you may still be spiritually dead. Those of us who have received the salvation God provides through Jesus Christ have been made spiritually alive. As Christians, we are no longer dead because of sin. But we are still troubled by sin. How can we handle temptation? Let's take a look at the way Jesus did it.

Matthew 4:1 When Jesus was about thirty years old, He began what is called His public ministry. He began to travel and teach. The first act of His public ministry was to be baptized in the Jordan river. Just after that, the Holy Spirit led Him out to the barren desert to be tempted by the devil.

Verses 2,3: After forty days and nights of fasting, anyone would have been looking forward to a great meal! Satan believed Christ would be weakened, so he took this chance to attack Him. That's lesson number one about temptation: Satan always hits you when you're at your weakest.

Verse 4: Jesus made it clear that He relied on God the Father for His needs. Satan will offer us the things of this world that seem most attractive—popularity, money and so on—in exchange for our loyalty to him. Just as there is nothing wrong with bread, there is nothing wrong with many of the things Satan offers—in the proper context. If they come before God in our desires, they are wrong. If we depend upon God, He will see that our needs are met.

Verses 5-7: Satan knew that Jesus had come to lead people to God, so he tempted Jesus to draw big crowds by performing some ridiculous feat of miraculous power. Perhaps Satan also hoped to place some doubt in Christ's mind about God's faithfulness. Jesus would have none of that. He believed God. We, too, need to believe that God is faithful to us and won't let us down. Don't believe Satan's lies that this world and his sins are better than what God offers. God loves you; Satan hates you.

Verses 8-10: Now Satan offered Jesus an easy shortcut to world domination—worship him and Satan would give Jesus all the kingdoms of the world. Jesus *will* rule this world—He won that right when He died for all of us on the cross. If Jesus had skipped the cross, we would all be forever lost in our sins.

Satan also wants us to worship him. People who have not received Jesus as Savior belong to Satan. Those of us who are obedient to Christ also have His power to say, "Away from me, Satan!"

Verse 11: Although the devil left Jesus at this time, he continued to plague Jesus throughout His public ministry. Hebrews 4:15 tells us that Jesus was "tempted in every way, just as we are—yet was without sin."

We can learn some important tips about handling temptation from this passage. First, Jesus was led by the Holy Spirit. We need to stay glued to God at all times. Only with God's power and presence can we hope to defeat the devil. Second, Satan attacks us when we are weak. Recognize what your weak areas are and ask God to take care of you there. Third, Satan doesn't tempt us with dull, boring things—He tries to grab us with nice things like money, fun, fame and so forth. But in the long run, these things are hollow and empty. Always keep in mind that Satan never gives away stuff for free. His price is a horrible one. (Do the Object Lesson here.) Fourth, Satan loves to make people doubt God and the Bible. If you have any doubts or questions, be sure to seek out the answers from a knowledgeable Christian. Finally, remember that God is much more powerful than Satan. If we stay close to God, we have nothing to fear from the devil. Jesus used Scripture to fight Satan. Reading the Bible and memorizing Scripture will help us in the fight against Satan. Temptations will never end until the day we die, but God is always with us to see us through.

OBJECT LESSON: FISHING LURE

Show your learners a fishing lure, the kind with plenty of bright colors and shiny surfaces concealing a nasty hook. Say something like this: **To a fish, this looks like the gourmet delight of the week. Unhappily for the fish, there is a hidden danger—a hook attached to a line attached to a pole held by a person who loves to cook and eat fish! The lure (an appropriate name) is really a deadly trap.**

In the same way, the temptations of this world are very attractive to us—but they conceal a deadly hook. If we bite into the temptations Satan offers, he will reel us in. Always remember to look for the hidden hook in the things of this world. Just stay close to Jesus and live the way He wants you to. You'll be all right then.

DISCUSSION QUESTIONS

1. **Why do you suppose Satan hates us and tries to trap us with temptations?**

2. **How can you tell if something you desire is not what God wants for you?**

3. **If you decided to give in to temptation, even though you knew it was wrong, what possible harm might result? Think of some specific temptations.**

THE COMPLETE
JUNIOR HIGH BIBLE STUDY
RESOURCE BOOK #11

Slave Bucks

This page features "slave bucks" that you can photocopy and give to your contestants. Place your own photograph in the center of each buck if you like. Add the name of your youth group or congregation. The Games and Things for Session 5 has a list of things players can do to earn bucks.

No Room to Boast SESSION 4

WHAT THE SESSION IS ABOUT

Salvation by God's grace leaves us no room for bragging.

SCRIPTURE STUDIED

Mark 12:38—40; Romans 12:3,16; Ephesians 2:6-10

KEY PASSAGE

"For by the grace given me I say to every one of you: Do not think of yourself more highly than you ought, but rather think of yourself with sober judgment, in accordance with the measure of faith God has given you." Romans 12:3

AIMS OF THE SESSION

During this session your learners will:

1. Discuss bragging and why no one has a right to brag before God;
2. Tell what pride does to a person's relationships with God and others;
3. Take a "pride" examination.

INSIGHTS FOR THE LEADER

Ephesians 2:6-10 is a natural continuation of verses 1-5. Paul began writing about our previous state of being dead in our sins, and how God had mercy on us and granted us life in Christ. Now he goes on to say how great our position in Christ is: God sees us as already in heaven with Him, and God is going to use us to display "the incomparable riches of his grace" (v. 7).

That sounds like we're pretty great stuff! We Christians ought to be able to brag a little about everything God has done for us—right? The Lord must think a lot of us if He did all this on our behalf!

No Boasting

Right—God does think a lot of us! But we're wrong if we think we have the right to do any boasting about it.

The Bible is very clear that salvation is a gift, unmerited and undeserved. We can be glad and grateful that we have it. But we cannot be proud of it. We did nothing to earn it; we simply trusted in what Jesus had already done for us. Verses 8 and 9 make this very clear: "For it is by grace you have been saved, through faith—and this not from yourselves, it is the gift of God—not by works, so that no one can boast." God did it all; we merely receive what He has done for us.

Verse 10 mentions "good works" which Christians are supposed to do as a result of salvation through Christ. Here is something different from simply trusting; this verse definitely talks about good actions. Don't we have some leeway to brag about the good actions we manage to do after we have been saved?

Again, no. There is never any room for pride in true Christian faith, because pride goes directly against God. Pride puts man in the place of God. Pride stiffens its neck instead of bowing its head.

Even the good works of verse 10 are God's from start to finish. To begin with, we ourselves are "God's workmanship"—or His work of art. We are what we are because He made us that way. And our good works are only the works God has already prepared for us to do. We can't brag because we are following the way He has laid out for us. "So you also, when you have done everything you were told to do, should say, 'We are unworthy servants; we have only done our duty'" (Luke 17:10).

Your junior high students are probably not in the habit of bragging about their salvation in Christ. It's very probable, though, that they are in the habit of bragging about something. And this passage from Ephesians teaches us that no one has anything to brag about when he or she stands before God.

Listen to your students as they come into the classroom. What do they talk about? Do they ask polite questions about each other's health? Do they offer to help each other with

problems? No, they're most likely talking about themselves—what they did yesterday, what they just bought downtown, what they've achieved since you last saw them (the highest grade in the class, the highest number of points in the game, the biggest laugh at a party). They compete for approval from you and from each other. They compete for recognition, for special honor, for position. Why? Because they are shy and uncertain of themselves.

Defusing Pride

Here's a fine line for the junior high teacher to walk. You want to build up your insecure students' self-esteem. You want them to know they're important to you and to God. If you never ask about their basketball games or their exams or their speech or band contests, you risk giving the impression that those junior high concerns are unimportant, and therefore your students are unimportant. The currency of junior high competitiveness may seem trivial to adults, but it is life to your junior highers. If your students are important to you, then you'll want to show interest in their concerns and praise their accomplishments.

And yet "no one can boast" before God (Ephesians 2:9). When are we building up our students' legitimate sense of worth, and when are we encouraging them to brag? It's not an easy question, but these might be a few helpful guidelines:

1. Congratulate achievers privately, one-to-one. Offering lavish praise in front of the entire class can be a put-down for the nonachievers and a puff-up for the achiever. Defuse pride by praising in private.

2. Praise honest effort as well as sparkling accomplishment. If your class has struggled to finish a difficult Bible study, don't just praise the "brain" who got done first; express your appreciation to everyone for trying and for doing his or her best.

3. Show approval when they do nothing as well as when they do something. If you give a hug or handshake for an achievement, give a touch on the shoulder now and then just because you pass a student in the hall. Try to show that your students are loved just for who they are, not because they have accomplished something.

SESSION PLAN

BEFORE CLASS BEGINS: Photocopy the Fun Page and the Bragopoly Teaching Resource game pages. The game pages must be taped together to form the game boards. Make enough game boards for each group of three or four students to have one. To play the game, students will need individual playing pieces (borrowed from board games or fashioned from twisted paper clips) and a paper clip and pencil to form a spinner as shown on the Bragopoly board. There is no Key worksheet this time. The CONCLUSION requires the use of index cards.

Attention Grabber

ATTENTION GRABBER (3-5 minutes)

Write this beginning of a sentence on the chalkboard or on a large piece of paper attached to the wall: "I hate to hear people brag because . . . ." As students arrive, ask them to complete the sentence. When all have arrived, read a few of the statements they have written. Then say, **We all agree that people who brag a lot are obnoxious and boring. But wait a minute. Do you and I ever brag about anything? Is our bragging any different?**

Discuss whether your own bragging is any better than or different from other people's bragging. (You may want to define bragging by explaining that it is the cheap road to recognition. Bragging says, "I'm wonderful," or "I'm better than you are." Recognition of one's own accomplishments is not necessarily bragging, but "puffing up" oneself to tower over others is.)

Say something like this: **There's a portion of Scripture that says no one has any right to brag in front of God. Let's look at Ephesians 2:6-10.**

ALTERNATE ATTENTION GRABBER (3-5 minutes)

When students have arrived say, **A funny thing happened to me on the way to class today!** Then make up a ridiculously arrogant story about your "mighty deeds" on the way to class (saving a child from certain death by stopping a runaway car with your bare hands, helping the fire department by putting out a huge fire, scoring the winning touchdown in "the big game" and so on).

After students begin to catch on ask them, **What am I doing when I build myself up with these absurd lies?** Someone may say, "You are lying." Agree, but say that lying is not the word you are looking for. When someone has guessed that you are bragging, congratulate them and say, **Most people brag—not with such outrageous nonsense as I was spouting, but with mild exaggerations or even with the truth. You can brag with the truth by continually reminding people of something you actually did. Whatever the case, bragging is obnoxious. Bragging is the cheap road to recognition. Bragging says, "I'm wonderful," or "I'm better than you are." Recognition of one's own**

NOTES

accomplishments is not necessarily bragging, but "puffing up" oneself to tower over others is. You might be interested to know that there's a portion of Scripture that says no one has any right to brag in front of God. Let's look at Ephesians 2:6-10.

Bible Exploration

EXPLORATION (35-45 minutes)

Step 1 (2-3 minutes): Since today's Scripture is a continuation of last week's, remind students of the topic you studied in the last session. (Christ has rescued us from death into life.) Then reread Ephesians 2:1-5 together.

Step 2 (2-3 minutes): Read Ephesians 2:6-10 to your class. To help them understand the passage more completely, explain the complex portions as you read.

Point out these main ideas of the passage: God sees us as being with Him in the heavenly realms—His own area—because we are in Christ. We are a display showing how great God's grace is, since by it He came to save sinners such as we are. He saves us by grace, we receive salvation through faith in Him. We are then God's "work of art," and we show we are saved by doing good works which God has already prepared for us to do.

Step 3 (8-10 minutes): Make sure everyone has his or her Bible open to Ephesians 2:6-10. Discuss the following questions with your students.

1. **According to verse 6, where are we in God's eyes?**
2. **What will God show through us, according to verse 7?**
3. **How are we saved, according to verse 8?**
4. **What does verse 9 say we can't do?**
5. **In verse 10, what are we supposed to do now that we're Christians?**
6. **Look at verses 9 and 10 again. Why is it wrong to brag or boast about our relationship with God (our salvation)?**

Read Mark 12:38-40 and Romans 12:3,16 to your students (or have volunteers read). Ask, **What is the difference between the spiritual attitude of the Pharisees described in Mark and the spiritual attitude of Paul (a former Pharisee) indicated in Romans?**

The Pharisees referred to in Mark 12:38-40 were proud of their self-righteousness and legalism, and they wanted other people to know what great guys they were. On the other hand, Paul calls for humility and a realistic assessment of oneself.

Step 4 (15-20 minutes): Guide students in forming groups of three or four. Give each group a Bragopoly game board, a paper clip and pencil to form the game spinner and enough playing pieces for each student to have one.

Have players put their pieces on the "Start" space and spin to see who goes first (highest number goes first). Allow students 15-18 minutes to play the game (they can play more than once).

Step 5 (8-10 minutes): Ask students some questions to help them think about the positive application of the Ephesians passage. Use the following questions or create your own.

1. **What do you think the attitude of a Christian should be?**
2. **What should your attitude be when you do accomplish a goal?**
3. **How is pride different from recognizing the talents and gifts God has given you?**
4. **Why is pride wrong?**

5. What effect does pride have on a person's relationship with God?
6. What kind of effect does pride have on a person's relationship with other people?
7. What are some of the end results of pride?
8. How can we guard against pride?

Make a transition to the CONCLUSION by saying, **We've seen that God has done some** wonderful things for us in Jesus Christ. But we've also seen that we don't have any right to brag or boast about our relationship with Him. Everything He has done for us is a gift. We didn't earn it and we don't deserve it. We should be humble, not proud, before God. And that means we should be humble toward one another, too. When we are proud, we need to confess it to God.

Conclusion and Decision

CONCLUSION (5-7 minutes)

Distribute index cards. Instruct students to individually construct a "Braggers Club Membership Card." Students can use their creativity to list four or more reasons why they should receive membership in the infamous Braggers Club. For example, they may write, "This person is a member in good standing because he takes great pride in his good looks." Or, "She thinks she's smarter than everyone else." Students may not tend to be quite that honest about (or aware of) their own faults, but encourage them to think of any area where they've made the mistake of being proud, arrogant or boastful. Be sure the students understand that no one will read what they list.

After everyone has had a chance to work for a few minutes, say something like this: **Now I want you to take a few moments for silent prayer to thank God for pointing out any problem you may have with pride or bragging. Ask Him to forgive you. When you are done praying, tear your Braggers Club Membership Card into little pieces and throw it away.**

Close in prayer.

Distribute the Fun Page take-home paper.

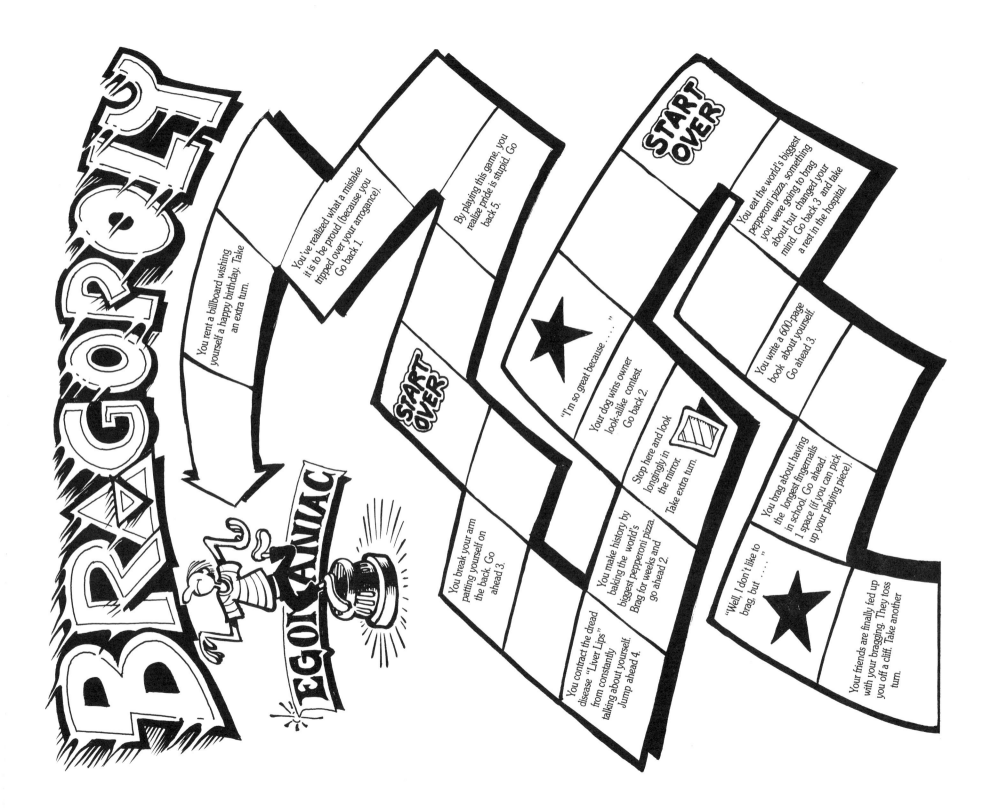

Your baby picture receives first place in an E.T. look-alike contest. Of course, this is something you won't brag about! Go back 4.

You are crushed under the weight of your own ego. Go ahead 1.

Your nose is stuck up so high it bleeds. Go ahead 3.

START OVER

Your head is so inflated you float up and get caught in the power lines. Go ahead 2.

"Everyone wishes they were me because . . . . . ,"

You finally saved up enough cash to buy those purple corduroys with 10 zippers on each leg and "Lulu" on the label. The day you wear them, they go out of style. Ego deflated, lose 1 turn.

You memorize 1,000 Bible verses and win a trophy which you proudly glue to the top of your head. Go ahead 3.

START

Instructions: Put all playing pieces (coins, pencil stubs, tiny cars) on "START." Spin the paper clip spinner as shown in the illustration. The player who spins the highest number goes first. Take turns spinning and moving ahead the indicated number of spaces. You must follow the instructions in the spaces you land on. Spaces that contain some sort of arrogant, prideful statement will cause you to advance toward the "EGOMANIAC" goal. Spaces with humble, proper statements will slow you down. First player to reach "EGOMANIA" is chief egomaniac—and the loser!

"Hollywood Star" squares: Anytime a player lands on a star, he or she gets to pretend to brag for 30 seconds. No one may interrupt, except with laughter. Any player who fails to brag must run around the room once screaming like a chicken.

TOWN CRIER

"For by the grace given me I say to every one of you: Do not think of yourself more highly than you ought, but rather think of yourself with sober judgment, in accordance with the measure of faith God has given you."
Romans 12:3

Based on Luke 18:9-14

JESUS PROMISES TO EXALT THE HUMBLE!

Story by ace reporter Typo

As Jesus spoke to a group of arrogant, self-righteous people today, He told a story about two men who went to the Temple in Jerusalem to pray:

"Two men went up to the temple to pray, one a Pharisee and the other a tax collector. The Pharisee stood up and prayed about himself: 'God, I thank you that I am not like other men—robbers, evildoers, adulterers—or even like this tax collector. I fast twice a week and give a tenth of all I get.'

"But the tax collector stood at a distance. He would not even look up to heaven, but beat his breast and said, 'God, have mercy on me, a sinner'" (Luke 18:10-13).

Jesus finished His tale by saying that the tax collector was the one justified in God's eyes, and that "everyone who exalts himself will be humbled, and he who humbles himself will be exalted" (Luke 18:14).

This reporter asked one of the men that Jesus had been talking to what he thought of Jesus' message. He said, "Get away from me, you scruffy little man. I haven't got time to talk to a worthless nobody like you!"

Oh, well.

Well, the infamous Acme Company has been at it again. You'll see what we mean when you read this actual advertisement for the all-new

ACME ELECTRO-GLORIFIER DEVICE!

Blows your own horn—for you!

Automatically positions your nose at the proper snooty level!

Holds your head up high!

Patented strain gauge (developed by earthquake researchers) measures swelled head!

Gyroscope keeps you constantly self-centered!

Loud speaker informs world of your accomplishments! (We provide taped message of wonderful accomplishments guaranteed to impress.)

Spotlight on you!

Makes sure you're always stuck-up!

Helium tank to inflate your ego!

Pats you on the back!

Hydraulic foot puts down other people!

Feeler gauge detects dangerous terrain, to protect you from what Proverbs 16:18 says: "Pride goes before destruction, a haughty spirit before a fall."

Pride is like a disease. Easy to get, hard to get rid of. Unhappily, there is no hypodermic shot-in-the-arm cure. Living a Christian life as God desires is the real solution. What does God think about pride? "I hate pride and arrogance, evil behavior and perverse speech" (Proverbs 8:13). Just remember that God is the One who gave you all the wonderful things about you. Praise Him and give Him the honor! That'll keep you humble.

▬ DAILY THINKERS ▬

Day 1 Read Ephesians 2:11-13. Write these verses in your own words. (Hint: The "circumcision" refers to the Jews.)

Day 2 Ephesians 2:14-16. Jesus removed the barrier between Jews and Gentiles. Do you feel hostility towards another race? Another church group? How can these verses be an example for you today?

Day 3 Ephesians 2:17. What kind of peace is

this? Is Paul speaking of in this verse? List other kinds of peace.

Day 4 Ephesians 2:18. According to this Scripture does God have favorites? Do you?

Day 5 Ephesians 2:19-21. If the Church is like a building, who forms the foundation? The cornerstone? The building itself?

Day 6 Ephesians 2:22. Once you become a Christian has God finished His work in you? How are you growing as a Christian?

Session 4

THEME: Self-centeredness.

BIBLE STUDY OUTLINE

Begin your message by doing the Object Lesson. Then read Luke 22:24-27 to your students. Make the following remarks as time allows.

Introductory remarks: We all have problems at times with selfishness and self-centeredness. We want to look and be like the flashy people in the flashy pictures. Would it surprise you to learn that Jesus' disciples also had the same sort of attitude?

Verse 24: It was the famous Last Supper, the meal that Jesus shared with His closest followers just hours before He was betrayed by Judas, captured by the soldiers and led off to trial and death on the cross. Somehow, during the dinner conversation, the disciples started arguing about who was the greatest among them. Can you imagine what a scene that must have been? Each person wanted to claim the credit as "Best Disciple of the Year." Maybe they thought Jesus was about to hand out trophies!

Verse 25: Jesus set them straight by telling them their behavior was like that of the unbelieving world. Those in authority loved to pridefully "lord it over" their subjects. They loved to call themselves "Benefactors." History shows that then, just as now, few people in authority actually spent much time trying to benefit others. They were in it for the power, fame and loot.

Verse 26: Jesus makes it clear that things don't work that way in His spiritual kingdom. Christians are to humbly and lovingly serve one another.

Verse 27: Jesus is our example of the servant-leader. He was obviously the leader of the disciples, yet He spent His time serving them in many ways. Elsewhere in the Bible (see John 13:1-17) it tells us that at this meal Jesus got down and washed His disciples' feet, a very menial task. This is the sort of Lord we have—one who cares for us and helps us.

It's not a part of human nature to want to serve others. Human nature wants to be served. But Jesus has taught us that being great means being a useful servant. Right after communicating this truth to His disciples Jesus did the greatest thing a servant could do. He gave His life for them—and for us.

OBJECT LESSON: PRETTY PICTURES

A grocery store magazine rack is a great place to find pictures of the "Beautiful People." Clip out a few photographs (after buying the magazine, of course!) featuring people who represent the world's standard of excellence: good-looking people, celebrities, rich people or political leaders. Christian magazines, especially those devoted to missionary life, are a good source of pictures featuring people who serve others.

Show your students the photos, contrasting the world's favorites with the simple servants. You can ask students to point out which people seem to be the most admirable. Chances are, their choices will be wrong. Say, **God doesn't look at the outside, flashy part of a human to judge his or her value. Let's take a look at a Bible passage that teaches us what God really does admire in His children.**

DISCUSSION QUESTIONS

1. **What are some things a junior higher could do to help and serve his or her school friends? What about at home with the family?**

2. **What are some ways we, as a youth group, can serve others?**

3. **What can you do when you feel that your outward appearance, possessions or level of popularity aren't flashy enough?**

4. **What happens when we measure a person's worth by what they own, look like or how popular they seem to be?**

Here are some ideas for slave party games. Masters send their slaves to participate in these games. Award ribbons or other prizes to the masters whose slaves finish first, second and third places. Adult sponsors can act as judges where necessary. Encourage masters to reward their slaves for their efforts by sharing refreshments and prizes with them.

SLAVE PAINTING CONTEST

Provide poster paints, brushes and clean-up items. Slaves paint portraits of their masters.

SLAVE WRESTLING CONTEST

Form a circle on the floor with rope or tape. Four slaves "wrestle" at a time. "Wrestling" is simply the act of pushing (without using hands) another person out of the circle. The last slave in the circle wins that heat; he or she goes on to the semifinals. The last three slaves to be pushed out of the circle in the final contest win first, second and third place prizes for their masters.

SLAVE CONCERT

The sample slave contract on the second Games and Things called for each slave to bring a kazoo or other musical instrument. You should also provide a few kazoos or plastic horns just in case. One at a time, the slaves perform "Mary Had a Little Lamb" or another familiar tune on their instruments. Slaves with percussion instruments can recite the poem as they play.

SLAVE JOKE CONTEST

Slaves come to the front of the room to recite a joke. Be sure to screen these jokes beforehand.

You might also try a chariot race (slaves tow masters on blankets), a dart gun target shoot, a pie-eating contest or any of a hundred other games that you'll find in the pages of this and other *Complete Junior High Bible Study Resource Books.*

Inner Strength

WHAT THE SESSION IS ABOUT

We must rely on God to give us inner strength and to change us from the inside out.

SCRIPTURE STUDIED

Isaiah 40:29-31; Ephesians 3:14-21

KEY PASSAGE

"But those who hope in the Lord will renew their strength. They will soar on wings like eagles; they will run and not grow weary, they will walk and not be faint." Isaiah 40:31

AIMS OF THE SESSION

During this session your learners will:

1. Locate, from selected Scriptures, key words about God's strength;
2. List areas of a person's character that God may create or strengthen;
3. Ask God to show His power in a weak area of their lives where they need it, or memorize Isaiah 40:31.

INSIGHTS FOR THE LEADER

Today's Scripture is a beautiful passage of good will. In it Paul expressed his hopes and prayers for the Christians at Ephesus.

The main theme of Paul's prayer for the Ephesians is power. Not the natural human power of being persuasive and successful; non-Christians could possess that kind of power. Paul prayed that the Ephesians would have the power of God's Spirit. It was that power which manifested itself in their values and character—an inward strength which would distinguish them from the society around them and would enable them to live as God's children. It would enable them to grow in grace and to develop maturity in Christ. It would enable them to grasp the greatness of God's love for them.

We've all longed for the power of the Holy Spirit—especially when we're faced with a difficult situation that has no apparent solution. Sometimes we wonder what's wrong with us because we can't seem to call on God's power to fix the problem immediately. We try, but often the situation doesn't work out as we think it should. Then we wonder if a lack of faith was the reason that God's power wasn't evident as we thought it ought to be.

God Gives Strength

There are certainly times when even those who have a good relationship with God can feel weakness and fatigue in their souls. At such times they can turn to the words of Isaiah: "He gives strength to the weary and increases the power of the weak" (Isaiah 40:29).

God is the one who firms our spiritual muscles and waters our parched spirit. "Even youths grow tired and weary, and young men stumble and fall; but those who hope in the Lord will renew their strength. They will soar on wings like eagles; they will run and not grow weary, they will walk and not be faint" (vv. 30,31).

The key here is setting our hope and reliance on the Lord. Since He is the one who is the source of power for humankind in the first place, He is the logical one to rely on for the internal strength to make it through the race with victory. Sadly, strength of character is not always considered to be of much value in the junior higher's world.

Many of your students are imitating someone they think that they would like to be; someone who has physical strength or power. But they don't realize that the strongest athlete and the most gorgeous actress will someday lose the skills or the looks that make them popular and give them a temporary power. The world's type of power is soon left behind.

Inner strength is an eternal commodity. It can be possessed by those to whom God does not give great attractiveness (by the world's standards) or physical strength. It can also be possessed by those to whom He does give

those attributes. It can be had by those of limited education or by those who are gifted as geniuses; it can be had in the ghetto or in a wealthy suburb.

Results of God's Power

Paul prayed for the power of the Spirit in the lives of the Ephesian Christians—but the power to do what? First, that they would be strengthened in their inner beings (see Ephesians 3:16). That kind of spiritual power is not the power to work spectacular miracles for show; it is the power of inner character. The Ephesians would win out over the pressures around them, not because they could destroy and dominate their enemies, but because they would have the inner strength through the Holy Spirit to withstand them. He would give them the strength to do the right things and to trust Him. That is a remarkable kind of power because so many people fold up when adversity comes along. The power of the Holy Spirit is the power of a strong inner character that can take it. Some of the elements of inner strength include honesty, integrity, kindness, unselfishness, self-control and discipline. Inner character is who we really are, not who we portray ourselves to be. It is the bottom line representing our values and motives.

Next Paul prayed that his readers would have Christ dwelling in their hearts through faith. By faith we first come into a relationship with Christ, and by faith we grow in that relationship, getting to know Him better and putting our roots down deep into the soil of His love. Faith is demonstrated by actions, and the actions that help us get to know Him better include regular reading of God's Word, prayer, fellowship, worship, obedience to the instructions we find in His Word and so on.

When we are rooted in the love of Christ, we will have the power to understand more completely how great His love is (see vv. 17-19). At the same time we will realize how His love "surpasses knowledge" (v. 19). Then we will "be filled to the measure of all the fullness of God" (v. 19). Our whole being will be flooded with an awareness of who He is in all His greatness and magnificence.

Paul's next mention of power is in verse 20. Here, at first glance, it looks as though Paul may be talking about the kind of power that we can use to accomplish the things we want. Doesn't he write that the Lord is "able to do immeasurably more than all we ask or imagine, according to his power that is at work within us"? Isn't that the sort of superpower we can call on to make life turn out the way we want it to? No, it is still God's power to use as God wants.

Notice that He can do more than we can ask or imagine. When we are done asking and imagining, God may do something very different and better! Our prayers, in fact, should focus on what God wills, not on our own desires (see 1 John 5:14,15). God wants us to come to know Him fully and to be indwelt by Him in such a way that we can understand the extent of what His love is doing in and through us. Only then are we in a position to recognize His power working through us.

The things God does will bring Him the glory that He deserves (see Ephesians 3:21). His power brings glory to Himself, not to us. He will not share His glory with anyone else. He will do great things in us and through us, but He won't do them to gratify our selfish desires. Instead, He'll do them to bring us and others to Himself in worship.

SESSION PLAN

BEFORE CLASS BEGINS: Photocopy the Fun Page. You must photocopy the Key worksheet only if you plan to do the first step in the EXPLORATION rather than the alternate suggestion. Make one copy for every two students (plus extras for any unexpected visitors.) If you choose to do the alternate first step instead, you need to do some special preparation as described there. You may wish to provide small rewards for the winners of the contests in the ALTERNATE ATTENTION GRABBER and the first step of the EXPLORATION. Poster boards or shelf paper and other materials are required in the EXPLORATION.

    SPECIAL NOTE: The next session, Session 6, is about Christian unity. The ALTERNATE CONCLUSION for that session requires students to bring plain T-shirts to class to paint with your youth group's motto or title. Be sure to tell this to your students at the end of today's class. You will also want to call students and remind them the day before you teach the next session.

Attention Grabber

ATTENTION GRABBER (3-5 minutes)

As students filter into the classroom, list these "superheroes" on the chalkboard: Superman, the Hulk, Spiderman, Luke Skywalker, Wonder Woman and Popeye. You can ask students to suggest others, but they must be characters with special powers beyond the ordinary.

Tell your students something like this: **Today I'd like to see how good your trivia memories are. I'd like you to tell me what it is that gives each of these characters his or her strength.**

Most of your students will have little problem matching Superman with the earth's sun, the Hulk with atomic energy anger, Spiderman with radiation, Luke Skywalker with The Force, Wonder Woman with Amazon magic and Popeye with spinach.

Explain, **We all realize that eating spinach doesn't have the same effect that Popeye always displayed and that there are no real secrets to strength and power that don't require hard work.**

Today we are going to take a look at a type of strength and power different from what we commonly consider. We are going to look at a strength and power that can increase over time rather than weaken, a power that can change what you are now and influence what you will become.

ALTERNATE ATTENTION GRABBER (5-7 minutes)

Challenge your students to a test of strength. Each person holds a book in one hand, arm extended away from the body and elbow locked. The person who can support the book the longest

without shifting or allowing his or her arm to droop is the winner. To be fair, all books should have the same weight. Use Bibles or hymnals.

Give the winner a small reward such as a discount coupon for your next youth event. Say, **Today we are going to look at a type of** **strength and power different from what we commonly consider. This strength and power can increase over time rather than weaken; it is a power that can change what you are now and influence what you will become.**

Bible Exploration

EXPLORATION (35-50 minutes)

Step 1 (10-15 minutes): Guide students in forming pairs. Ask them to look at the "Dig It Out" section of the Key worksheet. Explain, **Read the passages printed there and go through the word search puzzle carefully. Circle words you find in the puzzle that are from the Scripture passages. Be careful! The puzzle includes a test of how carefully you read the Scriptures. It contains some words that are not in the Scriptures. Do not circle those words!**

You can make a contest out of this activity by telling students that they will have a set amount of time to find the hidden words. Explain that you will give one point for each correct word and subtract two points for each word circled that is not in the Scripture passages. Award small prizes such as edible treats to the pairs that have located the most words. (See the copy of the puzzle on this page for correct words.)

After allowing time for students to complete the puzzle, regain their attention. Ask them to share some of the words they have found and to relate a sentence or two showing how each word is used in the Scripture passage. Use material from the INSIGHTS FOR THE LEADER for this discussion. This activity serves as an introduction to concepts that will be developed more completely as you move through the course, so it is not intended to be an exhaustive study.

```
E E P O W E R B K Y E B J G H F Y M B S O A R V X L L
K N E E L Z Q Z B C P Q Q T E W B E I N G X Z D G E R
D P P P Q Q Q M W M Z J H A Z Z H O L Y Q J W K N O
R X H O P E M Q Q Z I Z Z Q V J C Q J K L D E E P J O
X I X F Z E T T Q X K K E K Q H S T Q J J L Q O T
T X C Z R E N E W C I C G G N X X Z R J W A L K Y E E
E O Z H J B A Z F N Z Q Q S L O R D Q I Q Z F X X D
S X U G E X L Q A Z Q R U Z X E A G L E S Z P U Z F Z
T T G G Q S I M M Q Z Q Z S X L O V E J Z T E L Z A A
A X W W H Q V R I J E R U S A L E M Z J Q Q O L Q T M
B W E A R Y E Z L Z S P I R I T F F A I T H P N X H E
L W X Z Y J B B Y Z R I G H T E O U S J K K L E X E N
I P S T R E N G T H C H U R C H Z W Q H Z W E S P R Z
S D E C E I V E Q M E R C Y K K Q I Q E Z S K K X
H D M H E A R T S I M A G I N E X D R G Z A J J K Q Z
E J O Y F U L P O C E A N X Q Z Z E R H Z K X S O U P
D D S A I N T S N I N C R E A S E S R J Q T H T E N D
```

Alternate Step 1 (10-12 minutes): Before class, copy Ephesians 3:14-21 and Isaiah 40:29-31 onto a large sheet of poster board or butcher paper—but replace the key words (the ones in the "Dig It Out" word search solution on this page) with unrelated words of your own choosing. For example, the word "power" in Ephesians 3:16 could be replaced with "spinach." Tell students to look up the passages in their Bibles, figure out which words have been changed and list the correct words on a piece of scratch paper. Students can work in small groups or individually, whichever you prefer. Even students with other versions of the Bible should be able to create an acceptable list of words.

When most or all groups have finished, ask students to share the words they have found and discuss their meanings and importance, as described in the original first step.

Step 2 (15-20 minutes): Provide large sheets of shelf paper or poster board and felt pens to students. Explain, **Work together in your groups to brainstorm and list some characteristics you think would be representative of a strong inner person. Use ideas from the Scriptures we have studied and ideas of your own.**

After making your list, create a large ad for vitamins from heaven. Label your ad "Inner Being Vitamins." The term "inner being" is from Ephesians 3:16. In your ad describe what God can do for and give to those who allow Him to flood their lives with His power. You might want to draw a few sample vitamin tablets or capsules and label them with the characteristics that God's strength can provide in the lives of people your age. Help your students get started by suggesting Galatians 5:22,23 as an excellent list of characteristics God can build in a Christian.

Step 3 (5-7 minutes): Reassemble the class and ask students to display and explain their ads. Be sure to affirm them for their efforts.

Step 4 (5-8 minutes): Discuss the following questions with students as a transition to the CONCLUSION.

1. **What do you see as the source of strength that will enable a person to develop these qualities our class has listed?**

2. **How does a person receive that strength?**

3. **How does a person maintain that strength?**

Be prepared to give your own answers to these questions if students need help. The following brief ideas should help: Christ is the source of our strength. We receive and maintain that strength through our relationship with Christ, as we cling to Him, read His Word and live as He wants us to live. This implies obedience and growth in our relationship with Christ.

Conclusion and Decision

CONCLUSION (3-5 minutes)

If you have photocopied the Key worksheet, ask students to thoughtfully complete the "More Power to You" activity.

Otherwise, write Isaiah 40:31 on the chalkboard. Help students commit this verse to memory for use whenever they may need it. Have everyone repeat the verse and its reference aloud several times. (You can make this fun by having a shouting contest between two teams—if you happen to be far away from other classes!) Then erase the verse from the chalkboard (or a portion of the verse at a time). Ask students to repeat the verse and its reference aloud without referring to their Bibles.

Another way to do this CONCLUSION is to use a song that sets the words of Isaiah 40:31 to music.

If most of your students know the song, you can simply sing it two or three times to reinforce their memory of it. If most do not know it, teach it to them and explain that setting Scripture to music is a good way to memorize God's Word.

Close in prayer.

Distribute the Fun Page take-home paper.

If you plan to do the T-shirt painting as suggested in the next session's ALTERNATE CONCLUSION, tell students that they must be sure to bring a plain (one color, no designs) T-shirt to paint.

Be sure to call the students or send a mailer during the week to remind them about the shirts. You may wish to provide a few shirts for those who are unable to bring one of their own.

DIG IT OUT

"But those who hope in the Lord will renew their strength. They will soar on wings like eagles; they will run and not grow weary, they will walk and not be faint." Isaiah 40:31

Read the Bible verses printed below. Then search for and circle in the puzzle grid some of the key words from these passages. There are some words in the puzzle that are not part of the Scripture passages, so be on your toes. Do not circle those words! (Words may read across, down or diagonally.)

"For this reason I kneel before the Father, from whom his whole family in heaven and on earth derives its name. I pray that out of his glorious riches he may strengthen you with power through his Spirit in your inner being, so that Christ may dwell in your hearts through faith. And I pray that you, being rooted and established in love, may have power, together with all the saints, to grasp how wide and long and high and deep is the love of Christ, and to know this love that surpasses knowledge—that you may be filled to the measure of all the fullness of God. Now to him who is able to do immeasurably more than all we ask or imagine, according to his power that is at work within us, to him be glory in the church and in Christ Jesus throughout all generations, for ever and ever! Amen."   Ephesians 3:14-21

"He gives strength to the weary and increases the power of the weak. Even youths grow tired and weary, and young men stumble and fall; but those who hope in the Lord will renew their strength. They will soar on wings like eagles; they will run and not grow weary, they will walk and not be faint." Isaiah 40:29-31

```
E E P O W E R B K Y E B J G H F Y M B S O A R V X L L
K N E E L Z G Z B C P Q Q T E W B E I N G X Z D G E R
D P P P Q Q Q L M W M Z J H A Z Z H O L Y Q J W K N O
R X H O P E M Q O Z I Z Z Q V J C Q J K L D E E P J O
X I X F Z E T T Q R X N K K E K G H S T Q J J L Q O T
T X C Z R E N E W C I C G G N X X Z R J J W A L K Y E
E O Z H J B A Z F N Z O Q S L O R D Q I J Q Z F X X D
S X U G E X L Q A Z Q R U Z X E A G L E S Z P U Z F Z
T T G G Q S I M M Q Z Q Z S X L O V E J Z T E L Z A A
A X W W H Q V R I J E R U S A L E M Z J Q Q O L Q T M
B W E A R Y E Z L Z S P I R I T F F A I T H P N X H E
L W X Z Y J B B Y Z R I G H T E O U S J K K L E X E N
I P S T R E N G T H C H U R C H Z W Q H Z W E S P R Z
S D E C E I V E Q M E R C Y K K Q I Q I Q E Z S K K X
H D M H E A R T S I M A G I N E X D R G Z A J J K Q Z
E J O Y F U L P O C E A N X Q Z Z E R H Z K X S O U P
D D S A I N T S N I N C R E A S E S R J Q T H T E N D
```

MORE POWER TO YOU

Indicate, by checking the boxes below, areas in which you could use God's strength to build your inner character.

☐ **Care for the unlovely**

☐ **Responsibility**

☐ **Honesty**   ☐ **Courage to stand for what is right**

☐ **Attitude at home**

☐ **Correct priorities with time and possessions**

☐ **Self-control**

☐ **Consistency in my walk with God**

☐ **Other:**

Write a prayer to God asking for His help and strength in the areas of your life which you checked above.

TOWN CRIER

SAMSON, THE WORLD'S STRONGEST MAN, DIES IN BLAZE OF GLORY!

(If you call getting squished to death glorious.)

By staff reporter Typo
Based on Judges 16:23-31

Gaza—About 3,000 men and women attending a party in honor of a false pagan god were killed when Samson, the world's strongest man, pushed over a couple of pillars supporting the roof of a huge stone building. The structure collapsed in clouds of dust and rubble, flattening the crowds. Samson was also killed.

Samson's family came to pick up the remains for burial. I asked one of his brothers how Samson managed to become so strong.

"It was a gift from God. He also tried eating a lot of spinach, like Popeye. Too bad about his temper, though. Spinach always made him mad."

> "But those who hope in the Lord will renew their strength. They will soar on wings like eagles; they will run and not grow weary, they will walk and not be faint." Isaiah 40:31

JESUS PRAISES POVERTY-STRICKEN WIDOW!

By staff reporter Pifont

Based on Luke 21:1-4

Jerusalem—Eyewitnesses told this reporter: "As he looked up, Jesus saw the rich putting their gifts into the temple treasury. He also saw a poor widow put in two very small copper coins. 'I tell you the truth,' he said, 'this poor widow has put in more than all the others. All these people gave their gifts out of their wealth; but she out of her poverty put in all she had to live on.'"

Unlike the late great Samson, this woman had no unusual physical strength or power. But inside, in her heart where God looks, she had strength and beauty. And Jesus praised her for it.

WHY ARE YOU HOLDING YOUR **BIBLE** OVER YOUR HEAD AND STARING AT YOUR **WEIGHTS**, CHIEF?

OOPS! MY MISTAKE!

UGH! GRUNT!

WELL, AFTER READING YOUR STORIES ABOUT **SAMSON AND THE WIDOW**, I DECIDED TO LIFT WEIGHTS TO BECOME STRONG LIKE SAMSON AND TO **READ MY BIBLE MORE** SO I'D HAVE INNER BEAUTY LIKE THE WIDOW.

PUFF! PUFF!

WHAT'S THAT GOT TO DO WITH WHAT YOU'RE DOING NOW?

I GOT CONFUSED. I WAS LIFTING MY **BIBLE AND READING MY WEIGHTS.**

SLIP!

BONK!

UGH!

THE CHIEF MAY HAVE MESSED UP, BUT HE DEFINITELY HAS THE RIGHT IDEA, ESPECIALLY THE INNER STRENGTH AND BEAUTY PART.

I STRONGLY BELIEVE THAT THE BIBLE IS THE **KEY TO BECOMING THE BEST AND MOST WONDERFUL PERSON** YOU OR I COULD POSSIBLY BE!

I HOPE YOU BELIEVE THAT, TOO. PUT THAT BELIEF INTO ACTION. READ GOD'S WORD AND LET IT CHANGE YOUR LIFE.

"Search me, O God, and know my heart." Psalm 139:23

Most people care much more about their outward appearance than about what sort of person—good or bad—they are on the inside.

It occurred to us that a person could prove or disprove this point by watching a couple hours of TV and observing the commercials. Do most commercials appeal to the outward appearance, or the inward beauty? In other words, which matters most to the average person? Well, we are going to give you the chance to find this out. Using the survey below, a pencil, a TV and one to two hours of uninterrupted TV viewing you can conduct your own

SEARCH FOR INNER BEAUTY

As you watch TV, briefly list the subject and message of each commercial you see. After a full hour is up (or two hours, if you're into heavy, scientific research) complete the survey below.

How many commercials did you see? _____

How many tried to sell you something by using good-looking guys or girls? _____

How many tried to convince you that you would be happier if you bought their product? _____

Richer? _____ More successful? _____

How many tried to convince you that you deserve what they are offering? _____

How many implied that getting attention from the opposite sex will result from using their product or

service? _____

How many offered products or services that promised to improve your outward appearance?

Your inward beauty? _____

How many promised to make you into a kinder person? _____ More loving? _____

How many times did you see people doing or saying things that God would be sad to see you doing

or saying? _____

What do you think? Is the average person more interested in their outward appearance or their inward beauty? What do you think God cares about? Read 1 Samuel 16:7 and Galatians 2:6 to find out.

DAILY THINKERS

Day 1 Read Ephesians 3:1. Paul wrote the letter to the Ephesians from prison in Rome. Although you probably would not be put in prison for sharing the gospel, you might suffer in other ways. What problems might occur when you share the gospel with others?

Day 2 Ephesians 3:2,3. Do you feel that God's grace has been given to you for others? How could you put this truth into action?

Day 3 Ephesians 3:4-6. The word "mystery" is used here to mean a truth which was hidden before this time which can only be revealed by God. Underline the words which explain the mystery in these verses.

Day 4 Ephesians 3:7-9. Paul calls himself a servant of the gospel. Whom do you serve?

Day 5 Ephesians 3:10,11. What job is the Church given, according to these verses? How will this be accomplished?

Day 6 Ephesians 3:12. What enables you to approach God with freedom and confidence? Then, is there any topic that you could not bring to God in prayer?

THE COMPLETE JUNIOR HIGH BIBLE STUDY RESOURCE BOOK #11
©1989 by SSH.

THEME: Strength of Character.

BIBLE STUDY OUTLINE

Read John 21:15-19 to your students. Make the following remarks as time allows.

Introductory remarks: Peter was a very interesting disciple of Christ. He had been a strong, tough fisherman before meeting Jesus, and many times his rough personality caused him to make mistakes as he tried to live for the Lord. It took him years to finally become the sort of person God wanted him to be. In other words, he was a lot like most of us.

Verse 15: Jesus had been crucified and then raised from the dead. Now He appeared to His disciples and served them a fish breakfast by the shore. Shortly before His death on the cross, Jesus had told Peter that he would deny his Lord three times. Peter had said, "Even if I have to die with you, I will never disown you" (Matthew 26:35). Of course, Jesus was right and Peter was wrong. At the Lord's trial, Peter three times denied that he knew Jesus. He even called down curses on himself and swore at the people who questioned him (see Matthew 26:74). Now, in John 21:15, Jesus gives Peter a chance to reestablish their relationship. Peter agreed that he truly loved Jesus. In response, Jesus told Peter to feed His lambs—a reference to Peter's future spiritual leadership of the growing Christian body.

Verses 16,17: Twice more Jesus asked the question, "Do you love me?" and twice more Peter pledged his love. This was probably symbolic of Peter's three denials of Jesus earlier.

Verses 18,19: Now Jesus predicts the kind of death Peter would face because he chose to love and follow the Lord.

Tradition tells us that Peter was crucified. He made the authorities angry because he would not deny Christ and stop telling others about Him, so he was eventually put to death. Interestingly, tradition states, when Peter was faced with the cross he requested that he be crucified upside down—feet up and head down. Why? Because he didn't feel he was worthy to die in the same manner as the Lord he so dearly loved.

Peter's strong faith and steadfast commitment to Jesus—his strength of character—did not come instantly or easily. It took years of development. But by following Jesus even in the tough times Peter showed us the way to develop the Christian character we all need.

TRUE STORY: DROWNING BOY

Tell this story to illustrate the idea that following Jesus can be tough, but is always worth it in the end.

Two young boys were caught in a riptide and swept many yards out to sea. Unable to swim against the current, they quickly exhausted themselves in the powerful storm surf. Frightened and fearing for their lives, they told each other good-bye, thinking that they were about to die.

On the shore, a young man saw the trouble. He ran to his garage, grabbed a surfboard and paddled out to the boys. He placed one of the boys on the surfboard and began to swim behind it, pushing the board up the coast to get out of the riptide before heading to shore. But there was no room on the board for the second boy. He had to be left behind.

Then the man had an idea. He pushed the board several yards away, then shouted for the boy to swim to the board. Just before the boy got there, the man again pushed the board away and again shouted for the boy to catch up. By taking these small steps and by offering the board like a carrot on a stick, the man was able to lead the boy all the way to the safe shore.

In the same way, Jesus sometimes makes us follow some pretty difficult steps. It wasn't easy for the boy to keep trying for the elusive surfboard. But because he followed, he was saved. When we follow Jesus, even through tough times, He always leads us safely home.

DISCUSSION QUESTIONS

1. **To develop strong muscles, one must lift weights or perform other such work. What does this tell you about developing a strong Christian character?**

2. **What are some of the tough things in life that Christians your age might be forced to go through?**

3. **In what specific ways might these things develop your character or strengthen your relationship with God?**

4. **What advantages are there to having a strong character?**

Slave Contest Tips

Here are some important tips for running your slave contest. The Games and Things for Session 6 tells you how to run the party.

The contest should run five or six weeks, assuming your group meets two times a week. The slave contracts must be posted at each meeting. Time should be allowed at each meeting for adding signatures to the contracts, awarding slave bucks and totaling points. Plan on spending ten to fifteen minutes each time to accomplish this.

It is very important to impress upon your students that anyone who signs the contract is giving his or her word to show up at the party. If someone says, "Well, what if I'm sick and dying?" tell everyone that you will accept a note from Mom or Dad. It's a good idea to alert the parents to the contest rules and the party date.

You should view the contest as an important event. Keep your students' excitement level high by encouraging them to earn points and bucks. Because each team is involved in a struggle to earn points, you'll find that team members will encourage other students to get involved! Here are some ways contestants can earn slave bucks and team points:

Slave Bucks—Decide on the appropriate amount of slave bucks you wish to award to individuals for each of the following: attendance at meetings and special events; bringing a new person; being a first-time attender; signing the contract; bringing a Bible; bringing a Bible with the student's name on or in it; volunteering to read a Bible passage or answer a discussion question (slave contests work great for this!); wearing the youth group's T-shirt; memorizing a Bible verse.

Allow students to suggest "good deeds" they can do to earn slave bucks. (One youth worker had his car washed!)

Team points—Teams can earn a thousand or so points for accomplishing these tasks: having the most members in attendance; bringing the most new people to a meeting; signing up the most people; winning a game at a games meeting.

Announce the winning team one week before the party date. If necessary, inform parents of the results of the contest and the conditions their kids agreed to. You may need the parents' help to make sure the slaves show up at the party and keep their end of the bargain. Stress that the party will be a fun experience that they won't want to miss!

INSIGHTS FOR THE LEADER

WHAT THE SESSION IS ABOUT
God wants Christians to have unity.

SCRIPTURE STUDIED
Ephesians 4:1-6

KEY PASSAGE
"Make every effort to keep the unity of the Spirit through the bond of peace." Ephesians 4:3

AIMS OF THE SESSION
During this session your learners will:
1. Define the unity of the Spirit;
2. Rewrite Ephesians 4:1-6 in their own words;
3. Identify things that damage or promote unity.

Like most of Paul's letters, Ephesians divides into two parts: a doctrinal discussion (chapters 1-3) and a treatment of practical issues (chapters 4-6). With this session your students will begin their examination of the practical issues that concerned Paul when he wrote to the Christians in Ephesus.

"Keep the unity of the Spirit through the bond of peace" (Ephesians 4:3). Does that sound like the exact opposite of your junior high classroom? A typical junior high group is neither unified nor peaceful! They cut each other down, their minds go wandering off in all directions, they interrupt each other or they sit sullenly silent in their individual worlds.

Then what's all this in the Bible about unity? It seems impossible! It is possible, but only through the power your class examined in the last session—the power of the Holy Spirit. Such unity does not come naturally and easily, not even to mature adult Christians. It shouldn't be surprising, then, that junior highers have so much trouble with it.

As your students grow in the Lord they should learn that this is an area in which God confronts their natural selfishness. They want to do their own thing; God wants them to care about and support each other.

As their teacher, you can set an example of working toward Christian unity. Do you think of your relationship with your students as "me versus them"? If you do, pray that the Lord will turn your mind to think of your class as "us"! You are their teacher and you are in authority in the classroom, but you are also a fellow believer learning together with them.

Christian Unity
In today's Scripture there are four helpful things to recognize about Christian unity:

1. Being a Christian is a calling as well as a one-time decision to accept Christ. The Ephesian believers had already accepted Christ as their Savior. Paul urged them to "live a life worthy of the calling you have received" (Ephesians 4:1). A calling from the Lord is a continual challenge to our own will. To be called by Him means we have to keep listening to Him and rearranging our lives to follow Him. Your junior highers can expect God to confront them and ask them to make changes in how they think and live. God's call to unity, although it may go against their natural inclinations, is part of that holy calling.

2. The calling of Christ means putting others ahead of self. "Be completely humble and gentle; be patient, bearing with one another in love" (v. 2). Selfishness never produces unity, only chaos, because every person is out for number one. Christ has set the example of selflessness; as we follow His example we will promote unity. Remember, even He had to consciously submit His own will to His Father's will. (See Matthew 26:39,42.)

3. Unity requires effort. "Make every effort to keep the unity of the Spirit through the bond of peace" (Ephesians 4:3). Although spiritually we are one body (see 1 Corinthians 12), the practical demonstration of that oneness does not come naturally. It must come through the Holy Spirit. And it must come through our efforts. We have to keep at it, surrendering our selfish wills to His will and learning to work together in peace.

Oneness in the Spirit and the "bond of peace" mean that we Christians are "chained" to each other by our love, our patience and our willingness to overlook each other's shortcomings. We won't be pulling away from each other but working together. The tie that binds us is our care about each other, which develops not because we are good people but because God is working in us.

4. God already sees us as united. In His eyes our unity is already accomplished, even though we have the continual struggle of living it out. "There is one body and one Spirit . . . one hope . . . one Lord, one faith, one baptism; one God and Father of all" (Ephesians 4:4-6). Unity in Christ is not something we accomplish by gluing ourselves together. It is something God has already created and for which He has made provision in our spiritual lives. We have to rely on the Spirit in order to achieve Christian unity.

It is easy for junior highers (and the rest of us) to forget the Lord's concern about unity and oneness in our Christian fellowship. We tend to apply the values of the world rather than the values of Christ, even in the gathering of His people. Good-looking people are preferred even by Christians, and society's misfits are also misfits in most Christian groups.

Rude comments, pointed jokes and hostile feelings are unleashed with the same frequency in church youth groups as they are in school during the week. Cliques, pecking orders and cold feelings that have no place in the body of Christ nevertheless exist.

Steps to Unity

Your students will need to take active steps to build up the bond of love and unity within the group. They will need to be patient and understanding towards one another. They need to learn to enjoy the company of those whose hearts are set on God rather than those whose hearts are captured by the opponent. They need to learn that each person has value, and not to judge a person's worth on the basis of good looks or a bubbly personality.

They will need to learn to give of themselves (a difficult task for most junior highers since they tend to be takers rather than givers). They need to initiate conversations, be friendly to new people, talk to those outside their interest group and stretch to absorb more people into their circle of friends. Then they will be actively promoting the unity Christ wants to see among His followers.

SESSION PLAN

BEFORE CLASS BEGINS: Photocopy the Fun Page. There is no Key worksheet or Teaching Resource page this time. The ALTERNATE CONCLUSION activity is unique: your students are to bring in T-shirts to paint with your youth group's name or motto. You will need special paints available at hobby or fabric stores. Be sure to call or write students to remind them to bring shirts to class. The EXPLORATION calls for two large silhouettes of human bodies drawn on newsprint or butcher paper. Provide scissors for the EXPLORATION and the CONCLUSION.

   SPECIAL NOTE: The next session, Session 7, requires special preparation several days before class if you plan on using the ALTERNATE ATTENTION GRABBER.

Attention Grabber

ATTENTION GRABBER (5-7 minutes)

Lead your students in a discussion by using an example such as the following: **Suppose there was a basketball team composed entirely of players who only liked to dribble. What would be the results of having a team like this? Would you want to play with a team like this? Why or why not?**

Briefly discuss the need for teamwork and cooperation if a basketball team is to have any hope of winning.

Ask for definitions of the word "unity." Write them on the chalkboard and talk about them until you get a good definition which the class generally agrees on.

Say something like this: **Christians are like a team serving the Lord together. We need each other. We are all different kinds of people, but the Lord says we are supposed to have unity. Let's look at some Scripture verses in Ephesians that talk about the unity of Christians.**

Bible Exploration

EXPLORATION (30-40 minutes)

Materials needed: Two silhouettes of human bodies drawn on newsprint or butcher paper.

Step 1 (7-10 minutes): Each student (or pair of students) is to select at least one verse from

Ephesians 4:1-6 and rewrite it as if Paul were writing directly to your youth group. Paraphrasing a passage is an excellent way to check on your students' comprehension of the meaning of the verses. As they work, move from group to group, helping them with any parts of the passage they find difficult. If they seem to have missed the point of a verse, ask if they feel their wording means the same as what Paul wrote.

Have several students read their paraphrases. Summarize the passage and point out any insights your students have given. Emphasize that unity is not a request or a suggestion from God—it's something He insists on among believers.

Step 2 (10-12 minutes): Have students form groups of three or four. Say, **Work together to list things that may cause strife or division in the average junior high group. For example, making a rude comment about the way someone dresses would hurt a person. Think up some others.**

While they work, cut the silhouettes into separate parts such as head, right arm, right hand, left leg, left foot. Keep the parts of each silhouette separate. Distribute the parts of one silhouette by giving one part to each student. (Retain the parts of the second body for use in Step 4.)

Tell students, **Draw a quick pencil sketch of at least one of the things your group has listed. Or if you prefer, write a description of a real-life situation depicting something the group has listed. Draw or write right on the body part you received.**

Step 3 (8-10 minutes): Ask groups to show their work. Post the parts of this silhouette on a wall of the classroom, but do not assemble them as a unified body. This will illustrate the fracturing effects of the actions students have described.

Step 4 (5-10 minutes): Distribute the parts of the second silhouette. Tell students, **This time list some ideas for counteracting division and promoting unity. Put your ideas on the body part you have received. You can use the items written on the first body to give you ideas.**

Have groups share their ideas for overcoming division and promoting unity. This time, assemble the body correctly to show the unifying effect of students' suggestions.

Say, **It is very hard for some Christians to feel united with one another. Often the only time some people see each other is for a brief moment at a church meeting. It's hard to feel united with people when you see very little of them. Another problem is that we sometimes bring some of our non-Christian ideas about people with us into our Christian group— ideas such as jealousy, pride and so on. Let's consider how we are doing to promote unity with other Christians.**

Conclusion and Decision

CONCLUSION (8-10 minutes)

Direct the groups to read the Fun Page story and comic strip. Distribute scissors to each group. The first team to correctly assemble the puzzle on the page is the winner. The puzzle spells the word "love." Ask your students to describe a few simple ways they could demonstrate Christian love to others in the youth group.

Close in prayer.

ALTERNATE CONCLUSION
(15-20 minutes)

Materials required: Fabric paints in various high-fashion colors; paintbrushes; strips of stiff cardboard (for spreading paint across the shirt); fabric marking pens; tables on which to paint; wax paper to insert inside the shirts to prevent bleed-through; necessary cleanup items. Your students are to provide their own shirts, but have several extras available for those who cannot provide a shirt.

Tell students, **One of the forms that Christian unity takes in our group is the fact that we *are* a group. We are a youth group, with our own fun special events, Bible study meetings and the like. Today, let's make up a simple motto and simple graphic design that we can paint on our shirts. This way, we can wear our shirts and be identified as united members of this Christian body.**

Encourage students to keep their motto and graphic design *very* simple, such as a one- or two-color splash of paint labeled "Jesus is King." A good example of what we mean can be found in the "Clip Art and Other Goodies" section at the back of this book. The art can also be used as a letterhead to match the shirts.

Guide students in setting up the tables and paints properly. Walk around the room as students work, offering suggestions and encouragement. Be sure students clean the room thoroughly.

When through, give everyone a chance to view all the shirts. Ask your students to describe a few simple ways they could demonstrate Christian love to others in the youth group. Thank your students for their efforts and remind them that Jesus is the center of their unity and friendship.

The shirts will probably need several hours to dry. Tell students that you will be responsible for gathering the shirts after they dry and distributing them at the next meeting. (Be sure students label their own shirts.)

If you have class time remaining, allow students to quietly play the Fun Page game. Scissors are required.

Close in prayer.

If you haven't used it yet, distribute the Fun Page take-home paper.

NOTES

If you wish to do the next session's **ALTERNATE ATTENTION GRABBER,** you need to do a mailing to your students this week. See Session 7 for details.

Your students may wish to see this solution to the Fun Page game.

TOWN CRIER

"JESUS IS DEMON POSSESSED," SAY SCRIBES!

Based on Mark 3:7-11,20-26

Capernaum—Huge crowds from all over Israel had been following Jesus, watching as He performed miracle after miracle. Jesus healed many people, and whenever "evil spirits" (demons) saw Him, they would cry out saying, "You are the Son of God," as Jesus cast them out.

Most of the crowd admired Jesus, but some of those present were jealous of His power and popularity. And some even thought He was crazy! "He is out of His mind," said one close relative of Jesus.

A group of scribes—experts in Jewish law—came down from Jerusalem to see Jesus. They claimed that Jesus was possessed by Beelzebub (according to legend, Satan's right-hand man or Satan himself), and that Jesus cast out demons by the power of the ruler of demons.

But Jesus answered them and said, "How can Satan drive out Satan? If a kingdom is divided against itself, that kingdom cannot stand. If a house is divided against itself, that house cannot stand. And if Satan opposes himself and is divided, he cannot stand; his end has come."

Jesus' point was that His power was not Satan's, and that if Satan's forces were not united in strength, they would not have any power.

Satan is still our enemy today. As long as he and his armies remain united, they remain strong and dangerous.

But we Christians have God on our side. As long as we stay united—with God and with each other—we will be able to win the fight against Satan.

A FIREPLACE BURNS BRIGHTLY WHEN ALL THE LOGS ARE TOGETHER. SPREAD THE WOOD APART AND THE FIRE QUICKLY DIES.

IT'S THE SAME WITH CHRISTIANS. YOUNG OR OLD, YOU MUST REMAIN **UNITED WITH AND CLOSE TO** THE OTHER CHRISTIANS YOU KNOW.

TOGETHER YOU CAN HELP EACH OTHER GROW IN CHRIST. ALONE, YOU'LL FIZZLE.

OK, if you've read the *Town Crier* story, you know we are talking about unity—unity in Jesus Christ.

Please understand that being united with someone else does NOT mean being exactly the SAME as someone else! We can look different, talk differently, act differently, even think differently about certain things and still be completely united in our faith in Christ. We can be separated by time and distance and still be united in Christ. We are family.

Below is a bunch of weird-looking people, all separated and disunited. If you cut them out with a pair of scissors and put them together like a puzzle, you will notice that they spell a message.

The message is the answer to this question:

How do you spell "Christian unity"?

HEY! I FIGURED OUT THE ANSWER! I'M SO SMART!

IF YOU'RE SO SMART, HOW COME YOU'RE PLAYING WITH PAPER DOLLS?

"Make every effort to keep the unity of the Spirit through the bond of peace." Ephesians 4:3

DAILY THINKERS

Day 1 Read Ephesians 3:16,17. Where does Christ dwell on earth? How do others see Christ in you?

Day 2 Ephesians 3:18-21. Write words to a song which describe Christ's love for you.

Day 3 Ephesians 4:1-3. Underline the words which describe behavior worthy of a Christian. Which of these is easiest for you? Hardest?

Day 4 Ephesians 4:4-6. Find the seven things the word "one" (in some Bible translations, "same") describes in these verses.

Day 5 Ephesians 4:11-13. Why does God give apostles, prophets, evangelists, pastors and teachers to the Church? How can God use you for the same purpose?

Day 6 Ephesians 4:14-16. Using these verses as a guide, write a description of an immature Christian. Now write a description of a mature Christian. Does this maturity have anything to do with age?

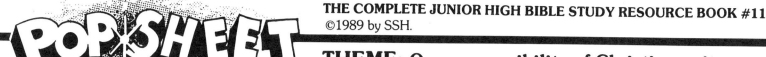

POP SHEET

Session 6

THEME: One responsibility of Christian unity.

BIBLE STUDY OUTLINE

Before reading 1 Corinthians 8:4-13 to your students, do the Object Lesson. Then make the following comments as time permits:

Verse 4: The people that Paul was writing to were upset. Some Christians had eaten meat that had been dedicated to a false pagan god. This sort of meat, which was some of the finest available, was often sold in the local markets after the pagan rituals. The problem was, some of the Christians saw no harm in eating this meat since there are no gods other than the true God; but other Christians thought the practice dishonored God. They were offended. To make matters worse, as we'll see in the following verses, the meat eaters continued to eat even though it offended some of their fellow Christians. They apparently didn't care that others were hurt.

Verses 5-7: Paul makes the point that there is but one God and one Lord—but some of the Christians of the pagan city of Corinth hadn't realized that the idols were not real. Their consciences were too weak to believe fully that God truly is the one and only God. Therefore, eating meat belonging to idols was to them a grave sin against Jesus.

Verse 8: Paul points out that meat has nothing to do with a person's relationship with Christ.

Verses 9-11: The real problem, Paul knew, was that weak Christians would tend to follow the meat eaters' example. They would try the meat, even though their consciences cried out against it. In this way, they would find it easier to disobey their consciences next time and in more important ways. This would lead to their spiritual destruction.

Verses 12,13: Paul took the mature attitude. Instead of telling the Corinthian believers that they needed to convince everyone the meat was OK, he told them they should abstain. Yes, it was technically OK to eat the meat, but if someone was hurt, then it was not right.

From this passage we learn a very important responsibility that we all have if we wish to be a united, happy Christian fellowship: Always think of the other person first. If what you want to do would cause another Christian to stumble into sin, don't do it. For example, you might think it's OK for you to miss Bible study a lot. But if in doing so you are teaching others that Bible study is not important, you are harming them. You should be an example.

OBJECT LESSON: HAMBURGER

Show your listeners a typical fast-food hamburger. Say something like this: **Did you know that a piece of meat similar to this caused a huge problem among Christians back in New Testament times? It's true! Let's take a look at "The Case of the Junk Food Furor" and you'll see what I mean.**

You can hold up the hamburger while you lead a study about the meat offered to idols.

DISCUSSION QUESTIONS

1. **Why do you suppose Paul chose not to tell everybody it was OK to eat meat offered to idols?**

2. **What did Paul see as the real problem?**

3. **What are some simple, practical ways we can put other people first here in our group?**

THE COMPLETE
JUNIOR HIGH BIBLE STUDY
RESOURCE BOOK #11

Putting the Slave Party Together

In this, the final Games and Things devoted to our slave contest, we offer some important tips and ideas to help you put the slave party together.

Because you announced the results of the contest a week ahead of time, the kids will know if they are to come as masters or slaves. Be sure to remind the slaves of the things they are expected to bring to the party and how they are to behave there. Food and other items that the slaves bring should be gathered in a central location in or near the slave party room as they arrive for the party. At least one adult sponsor should take charge of these items so that things don't become overly hectic when the slaves start serving their masters.

When ready to begin the party, take the slaves into a room just off of the area where the slave auction will be held. Two adult sponsors will be needed to prepare each slave for the auction. Another sponsor will act as auctioneer (get someone gregarious). Another sponsor can accept the slave bucks in payment. The youth leader, who can serve as master of ceremonies—controlling the flow of things—when the auction is completed. Just before beginning the auction, remind the masters of these items:

1. Masters can bid for slaves individually or in a group. Groups that own one or more slaves will need to share any prizes the slaves win.

2. When a bid is accepted, the slave bucks are immediately given to a sponsor. The slave will sit off to one side with other purchased slaves until the auction is completed.

3. Slaves are not to be treated harshly. (No carrying masters on their backs or use of demeaning language, for instance.)

4. A slave who refuses to obey an order is to be brought before a judge (an adult sponsor). The judge will decide if the order is reasonable. If it is, the judge will allow the slave an opportunity to perform the duty. If the slave refuses, the judge can order punishment.

Begin the bidding by bringing the first slave out in a trash can covered with a blanket. Only after the slave is auctioned can he or she be revealed. Masters may bid for slaves individually or in groups.

After the masters have received their slaves, herd everyone into the party room. Be sure no one sits in the center of the room, the area where the party games will be played.

Provide an official-looking robe and gavel for the judge. The standard punishment can be to chug-a-lug a can of cream soda, time spent in some cardboard stocks or a trip to the corner.

Remind masters that they are to sit back, relax and let the slaves do all the work. Give the kids time to have refreshments and enjoy themselves before beginning the games suggested on the Games and Things for Session 4. The party can go for about two hours. Photograph or videotape everything for posterity.

Maturity

WHAT THE SESSION IS ABOUT

The process of maturing as a Christian involves knowing and speaking the truth, growing in love, recognizing Christ as the Head and fitting into the Body of believers.

SCRIPTURE STUDIED

Ephesians 4:11-16

KEY PASSAGE

"Then we will no longer be infants . . . . Instead, speaking the truth in love, we will in all things grow up into him who is the Head, that is, Christ." Ephesians 4:14,15

AIMS OF THE SESSION

During this session your learners will:

1. Describe Christian maturity, based on Ephesians 4:11-16;
2. Identify marks of maturity and immaturity in believers;
3. Plan ways to act more maturely in one area of the Christian life.

INSIGHTS FOR THE LEADER

Maturity! If there's one quality that junior highers often seem to lack, it's maturity! Believe it or not, the Scripture says that your junior highers who are Christians are becoming more mature in Christ. You may not be able to see any progress, especially not at the rate you'd like to see it, but the Lord is indeed working in them. As they surrender themselves to Him, even in the smallest ways, He works to bring about maturity and growth. In His perfect vision He sees progress even when the rest of us miss it.

Christian Maturity

Ephesians 4:11-16 is about Christian maturity. Paul mentions some of the gifts Christ has given His people (to be apostles, prophets, evangelists, pastors and teachers—see v. 11) and why He gives those gifts—for serving one another in order to build each other up (see v. 12). As Christians help each other and build each other up, we are building toward something: "unity in the faith and in the knowledge of the Son of God" (v. 13).

In this "in-between" stage in their lives, junior highers often feel they don't have a place to fill in the Church or in society in general. They feel they're on hold. But God is working in them, and they are important to Him! He is causing them to mature and grow. Some congregations don't quite know what to do with their junior highers, so they leave them in a no-man's-land. Other congregations make a good effort to find a special place for their junior highers, and to recognize what they are doing. Students can help with midweek children's programs. They can read Bible stories to children when they baby-sit. They can give sermons in children's programs. They can help with ushering and other parts of church life. Take a look at how your congregation is doing in that area and consider what more could be done. At the very least your students can be special to you, their teacher, and can find a special place in your class.

Marks of Maturity

Verses 14-16 of Ephesians 4 give us several marks of a maturing Christian. We can measure ourselves against these marks and see where we still need to do the most growing.

1. Knowing the truth (see v. 14). A junior higher commented on something she had read in a magazine. When its truth was questioned, she said it had to be true because the name of the magazine was *True Detective*. A mark of maturity is the ability to sort out God's truth from the oceans of false ideas that surround us. It takes more than human intelligence to recognize truth. We need "the Spirit of truth" who will guide us into all truth (see John 16:13).

2. Speaking the truth (see Ephesians 4:15). Immature Christians will often tend toward some phoniness and pretense in their spiritual-

ity. More mature Christians can admit their faults, sins and struggles, knowing that God still loves them and is patiently working on them. Here is where you can set an example of honesty for your junior highers. By being honest with them about some of your failings, you can demonstrate that a maturing Christian speaks the truth without phoniness.

3. Growing in love (see vv. 15,16). Love means accepting people who are outside your usual circle of friends—learning to demonstrate and express your love rather than assuming that people know you love them (how often do junior highers tell Mom and Dad "I love you"?). Love means caring about the less attractive people and the misfits of the world. It means developing care and concern for people you've never met—the hurting, starving people of the world. Love means seeing yourselves as possible resources to take away some of that hurt.

Your example is also important to your students' development of love. Thorough Bible knowledge and excellent methods and facilities will fall flat if you do not genuinely care for your students; and if you care about them, it's possible to overcome poor facilities and have an excellent class.

4. Recognizing Christ as the Head (see. v. 15). When we are maturing Christians we recognize our limitations; we know we have to rely on the Lord. He provides the direction we need. In a healthy body the head provides the information that is needed for movement and for accomplishing the various tasks that the body is capable of doing. If something goes wrong in the head or in the ability of nerves and muscles to respond to directions, the results are sad—spastic disorders, seizures, paralysis, blindness and so on. Similarly, the Body of Christians needs to respond to the directions given by our Head. The

more completely we respond, the more coordinated and effective is the Body, and the better able it is to do what it should be doing for Him in the world.

As we mature, we are growing in Christlikeness. Our aim as Christians—what we are growing toward—is not bigger and better programs or a more successful ministry; our aim is being closer to Christ. If He comes first in your efforts to help young people, you're on the way to help produce mature Christians.

5. Fitting into the Body and doing our part (see v. 16). Mature Christians recognize that Christians are all one Body and that they need each other. Mature believers look for their proper and useful place in the Church and pull their own weight. They know they need other believers; they also seek to help other believers who need them. Your junior highers will take a big step of maturity when they stop wanting to be just entertained, and start looking for ways they can help their congregation.

It's very important to remember that the source of Christian maturity is faith and the knowledge of the Son of God (see v. 13). Christian growth comes through trusting the Holy Spirit rather than merely through efforts to do better. A mature Christian is one who is mature in faith, rather than one whose actions are flawless.

If students are using Bible versions that use the word "perfect" in verse 13, point out the following information. In the original language, the word "perfect" (*teleios*) means complete, finished, fulfilling the purpose for which it was intended. What is God's purpose for us? That we will put our faith and trust in Him; that we will rely on Him and depend on Him. A mature Christian depends less and less on his or her own abilities or goodness and more and more on the Lord's guidance and mercy.

SESSION PLAN

BEFORE CLASS BEGINS: Photocopy the Key worksheet, the Fun Page and both pages of the Teaching Resource game, which must be assembled into game boards after copying. You should make two or three copies of the game for every group of four students (so groups can play several times if they like). Each player in a group needs a color that is different from the rest of the players in his or her group. The ATTENTION GRABBER and ALTERNATE ATTENTION GRABBER call for special materials. The ALTERNATE ATTENTION GRABBER requires special preparation several days before class. Refer to the activities below for further information.

Attention Grabber

ATTENTION GRABBER (8-10 minutes)

Materials needed: magazines, scissors, construction paper and glue.

Direct students to assemble into groups of three to five. Explain, **I want each group to create a work of art. Your job is to cut out at least three photos from the magazines and assemble parts of these photos to create one picture. Your picture will illustrate the most mature–looking individual you can make. Glue the various pieces to the construction paper. You have about six minutes to work.**

If anyone asks what you mean by "mature," tell them that's for them to decide.

When time is up, gather and display the students' efforts. Ask each group to explain what they were trying to communicate with their posters. Some groups will have tried to make people who look very old. One or two groups may have done something clever like putting two heads on one neck to symbolize the part that wisdom and intelligence play in maturity. Other groups may have given up in frustration and just assembled something

meaningless (which also teaches something about maturity—or the lack of it).

Say, **Today we are going to take a look at a portion of Ephesians that teaches us about Christian maturity. Christian maturity is different from what we've seen on these posters. Let's open our Bibles and see what we can learn.**

ALTERNATE ATTENTION GRABBER (5-7 minutes)

Materials needed: Inexpensive child's jigsaw puzzle, white spray paint, permanent felt marker, envelopes, postage stamps.

Preparation: Several days before you teach this session obtain a jigsaw puzzle that has at least as many pieces as you have students. Put the puzzle together and spray paint it white. With a permanent felt marker write a message concerning this session such as, "Maturity: How do you know if you have

NOTES

it?" or, "Can this puzzle be perfect if there are missing pieces?" Mail a piece of the puzzle to each student several days before class with a note encouraging him or her to bring the piece to the next class.

As students arrive, have them put their puzzle pieces together (including the left-over pieces which you have brought) and try to make out the message of the puzzle.

If one or more pieces are missing say, **Today we are going to take a look at a subject that resembles this puzzle. It's Christian maturity. In our hearts we have some of the pieces of maturity, but most of us are still missing a few to be completely mature.** Reveal the puzzle's message if it is not discernible.

If all the pieces show up, say something like this: **This puzzle illustrates something that we are going to be considering today—getting all the pieces together in our lives. It's also called Christian maturity—growing spiritually and doing the wise and right thing.**

Bible Exploration

EXPLORATION (35-45 minutes)

Materials needed: "The Road to Maturity Game!" Teaching Resource pages, colored pencils (in assorted colors), Key worksheet.

Step 1 (12-15 minutes): Guide students into groups of two or three (or have them work individually if the class is small). Have them complete the "Maturity: Do You Have It?" section of the Key worksheet. When they have completed the study, regain their attention and have them report their answers. Discuss their responses, using material from the INSIGHTS FOR THE LEADER to help them understand Christian maturity. Reiterate the points that maturity involves knowing and speaking the truth, being loving, recognizing Christ as the Head and fitting into the Body and doing our part.

If any students are reading a Bible version that uses the idea of "perfection" in the study passage, point out the "Who's Perfect?" section of the Key.

Step 2 (15-20 minutes): Assemble groups of three or four students. Give each group a copy of the "The Road to Maturity Game!" Every player in a group must have a colored pencil; the pencil lead must be a different color for each player in a group.

Read the instructions printed on the game. Be sure students understand that a player cannot draw a line twice through an intersection, even if the lines don't touch. (This is how most mistakes are made.) The following illustration shows what can and cannot be done.

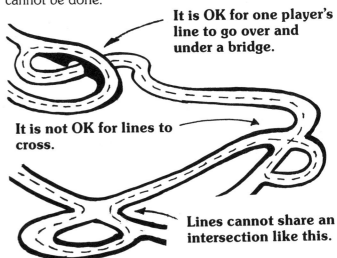

It is OK for one player's line to go over and under a bridge.

It is not OK for lines to cross.

Lines cannot share an intersection like this.

Let students play the game. Encourage groups to play as many rounds as they can before time is called. Have plenty of extra game boards on hand so each group can have a new one for each round.

Step 3 (7-10 minutes): Reassemble the class and ask students how many points they managed to score. Congratulate the highest scorer.

Say, **Most of the ideas of maturity on the game board were taken from the Bible. Let's see if you've learned something about the Bible's view of maturity.** Discuss the following questions; spend several minutes on the final two questions.

1. **How would you define "maturity", in a few words, according to what the Bible says?**

2. **What are some ways that people might show they are not mature in their Christian faith?**

3. **What are some ways people demonstrate Christian maturity?**

Make a transition to the CONCLUSION by saying, **We are taking a look at Christian maturity today. It is not something that a person gets instantly upon reaching a certain age. In fact, each of us is constantly maturing in his or her outlook on things and in his or her walk with the Lord. Let's take a moment and see if there are some things that we could do to mature or grow up a little more this week.**

Conclusion and Decision

CONCLUSION (5-10 minutes)

Tell students to complete "A Mature Prayer" on the Key worksheet. They will not have to show their work to anyone.

Close in prayer, asking God to help each of you depend on Him for spiritual growth.

Distribute the Fun Page take-home paper.

MATURITY: DO YOU HAVE IT?

Believe it or not, if you are a Christian God is working in you right now to make it happen!

1. According to Ephesians 4:11-13, why does Christ give certain abilities to certain people?

   What does Christ want us to become and attain, according to verse 13?

2. Verse 14 talks about "waves" and "wind." But it doesn't mean physical waves and wind as on an ocean. Say in your own words what it's really talking about.

3. According to verse 15, how does a mature Christian talk?

   When a Christian tells a lie, what does that tell you about his or her maturity?

4. What do you think verse 15 means when it says Christ is our "Head"?

5. According to verse 16, we are all part of one Body, the Body of Christ. What is each part of the Body supposed to do?

6. What happens when each part of the Body does what it should do?

> *"Then we will no longer be infants . . . . Instead, speaking the truth in love, we will in all things grow up into him who is the Head, that is, Christ."*
> *Ephesians 4:14,15*

WHO'S PERFECT?

Does your Bible use the word "perfect" or "perfection" in Ephesians 4:13? Sounds impossible, doesn't it? In the original language of the New Testament (Greek), that word means complete, finished, mature, fulfilling the purpose it's meant for. God's main purpose for you is that you'll have faith in Him, that you'll learn to trust in, rely on and depend on Him. So a "perfect" Christian is one who is complete in trusting the Lord—not one who always does everything exactly right.

A MATURE PRAYER

An area in which I need to be more mature (grow up) in my relationship with God:

My prayer for help:

Here's one thing I will do to show more maturity in that area of my life:

THE ROAD TO MATURITY GAME!

Materials needed: As many different colors of pens or pencils as there are players in a group.

Instructions: The object of the game is to pick up as many "maturity points" as possible. (Some of the maturity points are based on Ephesians 4:14-16 and other parts of the Bible, some are general marks of maturity.)

Players pick up points by traveling down the roads with their pens or pencils. **BUT: No player may cross his or her own path or use the same road twice. A player cannot use the same intersection more than once, even if his or her lines don't touch.** However, paths can be crossed over or under bridges.

Each player plays the game in turn, trying to earn the most points. Each player starts at the sign marked "Begin" and finishes when no unused roads are available. (Of course, roads used by other players in previous turns may be used again by each new contestant.)

If time permits, players may play again on a new game board. The player who ultimately finds the highest scoring path is the winner.

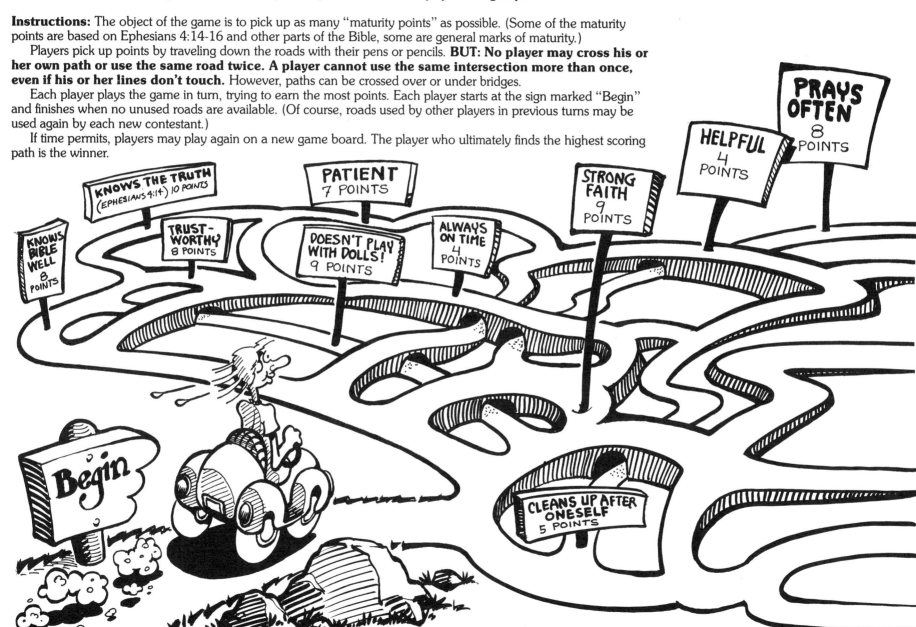

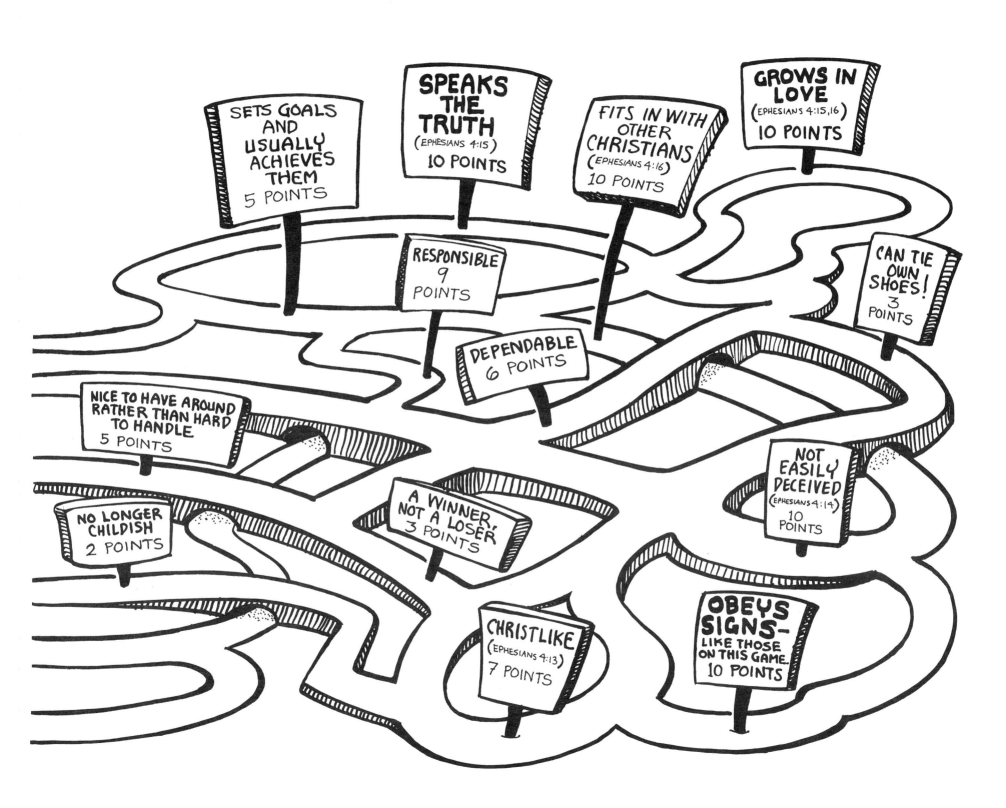

TOWN CRIER

"Then we will no longer be infants. . . . Instead, speaking the truth in love, we will in all things grow up into him who is the Head, that is, Christ."
Ephesians 4:14,15

AND SO...

BOYS, I'VE RECEIVED A PHONE CALL FROM **PROFESSOR E. EMSIE SQUARE.** HE CLAIMS HE'S INVENTED A **SECRET** FORMULA TO MAKE PEOPLE INSTANTLY **MATURE.** GO CHECK IT OUT.

RIGHT.

YES! I, THE GREAT PROFESSOR E. EMSIE SQUARE, HAVE CREATED MY GREATEST INVENTION OF ALL TIME!!

ONE SWALLOW OF MY SECRET FORMULA, AND I WILL BECOME THE WORLD'S MOST **MATURE** PERSON!!! I WILL BE **ADULATED** BY THE PEOPLE OF THE WORLD!!

ADULATED?

DON'T ASK ME.

ADULATE (ăd'jə lāt') v.t. [i. adulatus, past part. of adulari] TO FLATTER IN A SERVILE WAY; TO PRAISE OBSEQUIOUSLY.

WATCH CLOSELY, FOOLS. I WILL NOW SWALLOW MY FORMULA. BEFORE YOUR VERY EYES I WILL BE INSTANTLY TRANSFORMED INTO THE ULTIMATE IN MATURITY!

COMPARED TO ME, THE PEOPLE OF THE WORLD WILL BE MERE **CHILDREN!** I'LL **ENSLAVE** THEM ALL! I'LL RULE THE EARTH! I'LL BECOME EMPEROR SQUARE, KING OF THE UNIVERSE!!

ONE HOUR LATER...

HMMM.... NOTHING YET.

TIC TIC

ONE MINUTE LATER...

ONE WEEK LATER...

WELL?

BE PATIENT. IT'S JUST TAKING LONGER THAN I THOUGHT.

Z-Z-Z

ONE YEAR LATER...

BY CRACKIE, HE'S RIGHT!

I'VE GOT TO ADMIT, HE **DOES** LOOK MORE MATURE!

WHERE'D I PUT MY DENTURES?

50 YEARS LATER...

SEE!? I TOLD YOU IT WOULD WORK!

YOU'RE 51 YEARS, 7 DAYS, AND 61 MINUTES PAST DEADLINE!!

MANAGING EDITOR

THE "BOYS" RETURN TO THE CHIEF...

NICE STORY, GUYS. JUST ONE PROBLEM.

WHAT'S THAT, CHIEF?

CONTRARY TO POPULAR BELIEF, MATURITY SOMETIMES HAS LITTLE TO DO WITH BEING OLD. SOME OLDER PEOPLE REMAIN CHILDISH AND SOME CHILDREN SEEM WISE BEYOND THEIR YEARS. TO BE MATURE MEANS TO BE COMPLETE OR FULLY DE-VELOPED. FOR CHRISTIANS IT MEANS TO BE LIKE JESUS. FOR MORE ON THIS, READ **EPHESIANS 4:14-16!**

Christian maturity, according to Ephesians 4:14-16, involves these things:

Knowing the truth. In other words, allowing the Holy Spirit to guide us in all truth (see John 16:13).

Speaking the truth. That means no game playing. Always honest with God, yourself and others.

Growing in love. The kind of love that cares for unlovely people, and the desire to do whatever possible to help others.

Allowing God to be our Head, our final authority.

Christlikeness. Jesus was not some wimp in a white bathrobe. He is the ultimate example of the very finest things a person can be.

Working together with other Christians—as a habit, not just twice a year. You are becoming mature when you stop wanting to be only entertained by your minister or teacher and start wanting to help out.

OK, so how do you become a mature Christian? Simple! You just decide for yourself you are going to try to do everything mentioned in the list above, and then you do it—always with Jesus Christ's help and power, of course. Well, to be perfectly honest (point two in our list!) there may be just one more little thing to consider.

To find out an additional very important idea behind successful maturity, work out the rather difficult word game below. The answer is printed at the bottom of the page.

L + ☺ - S + 🖼 - LE - S + 🍷 - LE + 🐍🐍🐍 - LRANDONIONS! + 👤 - CK - NAKE = ❓

I CAN'T STAND —

I FEEL !

━ DAILY THINKERS ━

Day 1 Read Ephesians 4:17,18. Non-Christians search for answers to life's problems in the wrong places. Paul calls this "the futility of their thinking." Make a list of these dead-end answers. (Example: cults.)

Day 2 Ephesians 4:19. What is the result of separation from God? What one word describes this?

Day 3 Ephesians 4:20,21. Underline the word used to describe Jesus in verse 21. How

has this characteristic of Jesus made a difference in your life?

Day 4 Ephesians 4:22-24. How does Paul describe the old self? How does he describe the new self? Which one resembles you?

Day 5 Ephesians 4:25. Why are you to be truthful?

Day 6 Ephesians 4:26. How can anger lead to sin? What are some acceptable ways you can deal with anger?

The answer to our picture game is "sticktoitiveness" (L + STAMP - LAMP + SICK - S + TOILET - LE + LIVER AND ONIONS - LRANDONIONS + NECK - CK + SNAKES - NAKE = STICKTOITIVENESS) which is a genuine word from the dictionary (some dictionaries add hyphens to the word). In this case it means that a mature Christian is one who constantly and without wavering follows the list we have at the top of this page. How's your sticktoitiveness? It'll get better the more time you spend sticking to Jesus.

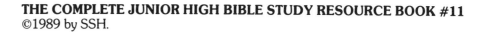

THEME: Some signs of maturity.

Session 7

BIBLE STUDY OUTLINE

Read Luke 16:10-12 to your students. Begin your message with the skit, then make the following remarks as time allows.

Introductory remarks: What a great skit! The seeker was looking for some tips about growing up and being mature. We'll find some tips for becoming mature by going to the truly wisest person of them all: the Lord Jesus.

Verse 10: Here is a basic yet profound principle of maturity: If you can handle small responsibilities, you'll eventually be able to handle the big jobs. On the other hand, if you are developing the habit of not being responsible now, you will continue to have trouble handling future responsibilities.

Verse 11: The Lord points out that, naturally, if you are an irresponsible person, no one's going to trust you with important things. The Lord uses the example of money to illustrate this principle of maturity, but His principle applies to all areas of responsibility.

It's not hard to see which of us are the mature ones and which of us are the immature ones. You can tell by who cleans up after themselves and who leaves the messes. Maturity is evident in the actions of a person.

Verse 12: This is one of the outstanding signs of a mature person: The ability to take care of another person's property. You can tell how grown-up a person is in this area by the condition in which he or she leaves this room, the way the person treats our van and the way the person picks up after him- or - herself at any of our special events. You yourselves may have had the sad experience of lending a friend something of importance, only to have it returned damaged or dirty. That friend has acted immaturely.

Do you want to be mature and grown-up? Here, based on the Lord's simple principles in this passage, are some of my own suggestions:

1. If you borrow something, return it. If you lose it, replace it. If you break it, fix it. If you get it dirty, clean it up. Say, "Thank you."

2. If you tell someone you are going to do something, do it. Do it on time. If you can't do it, warn them in advance.

3. Don't be afraid to apologize if you make a mistake. People need to hear apologies.

These are just a few things a mature person does. You can probably add more ideas to the list, too. If you were listening carefully, you might have been comparing yourself to the list. I hope you compare favorably.

SILLY SKIT: GURU TO YOU, TOO

This silly skit will get a smile from your listeners and help focus their attention on the subject of growth and maturity. You can play the part of the Narrator and the Seeker; another person should be the Guru. Overacting is the key to success!

Narrator: After searching the world for many years, a young man [or woman] has finally come to his final destination in his quest for truth—his hunt for wisdom and knowledge. Struggling to the top of the highest peak in exotic India, he finally comes to the supposedly wisest man on earth, Guru Bob. The young seeker is searching for the knowledge of maturity and personal growth. What will be the guru's wisdom on the subject of growth?

Seeker: Teacher, I have searched, lo, these many years to ask you this one most important question: What is "growth"?

Guru (in lotus position and speaking with Indian accent): My son—or daughter, whichever you may be (I've lost my glasses)—it is a group of trees standing together without underbrush; it is a small forest; it is . . .

Seeker: Excuse me—that's "growth"?

Guru: Oh, "growth"! I thought you said "grove."

DISCUSSION QUESTIONS

1. **Besides being responsible, what other personality traits might a mature person display?**

2. **How can a person develop some of these traits as habits?**

3. **What advantages are there to being mature?**

Things to Do with Squeeze Bottles—Outdoors, and in Clothes That Water Won't Ruin!

LIQUID REFRESHMENT

Place several water-filled squeeze bottles in a circle marked on the ground. The circle should be 3 or 4 feet across. Have extra squeeze bottles and a source of water to replenish the bottles in the circle as they are used up.

Gather players into two or more teams. At a signal, the first player from each team runs from a starting point into the circle, grabs a bottle and starts drenching the other player(s). The first player to empty the bottle scores a point for his or her team. The players go to the end of the line of their teams while new players play a second round. Leaders replenish the squeeze bottles between rounds. Play as many rounds as you like, until everyone is thoroughly wet.

QUICK DRAW

This is similar to the above game, but plays more quickly. Form two teams. Separate the teams by several yards and place two squeeze bottles at the center point between them. Count off the players with numbers. When you call a number, the player from each team with that number runs, grabs a bottle and sprays the other player. A leader watches carefully to see who scores the first hit. The successful player receives a point for his or her team.

RUSSIAN WATER ROULETTE

This game works best for small groups. Seat everyone in a circle on the ground. The leader holds a squeeze bottle fairly close to the face of one player. An assistant flips a coin and calls out the results—heads or tails. If it's tails, the leader does nothing except move on to the next player. If the coin lands heads, the leader squirts the player in the face. That player is "dead" and leaves the game. The leader goes around the circle, squirting any unlucky player until only one player is left. Then, if you are daring enough, provide squeeze bottles for players to drench the leader.

The New Self

WHAT THE SESSION IS ABOUT

The difference between the darkness of the world's perceptions and the light of Christ.

SCRIPTURE STUDIED

Psalm 73:1-6,16-19,23,24,28; Ephesians 4:17-24

KEY PASSAGE

"You were taught, with regard to your former way of life, to put off your old self, which is being corrupted by its deceitful desires; to be made new in the attitude of your minds; and to put on the new self, created to be like God in true righteousness and holiness." Ephesians 4:22-24

AIMS OF THE SESSION

During this session your learners will:

1. Examine some problems nonbelievers face;
2. Discuss the benefits of being Christian;
3. Have an opportunity to make and renew their commitments to God.

INSIGHTS FOR THE LEADER

The first part of today's Scripture passage from chapter four of Ephesians is full of negative words: futility, darkened, ignorance, hardening of their hearts, lost all sensitivity, sensuality, impurity and lust. All those words describe the person "separated from the life of God" (v. 18). It is certainly an unattractive picture of a non-Christian!

Picture of Darkness

Notice some of the words the Holy Spirit caused Paul to use. Futility—a word that describes the lives of many nonbelievers. A person whose life's direction is in the end meaningless may not be a "bad" person. He or she may have ethics and morals, but the total sum of his or her life's energy adds up to nothing. He or she has contributed nothing of eternal value. This sort of life reflects the familiar Christian saying, "Only one life 'twill soon be past, only what's done for Christ will last."

Darkness and ignorance are also very descriptive of the thinking of a person without Christ. This is not to say that Christians are more intelligent than others, nor to imply that non-Christians are incapable of making sound and even morally correct decisions. But the base from which a person makes those decisions is usually inadequate in those who do not hold to God's truth. Even Christians themselves can act in a darkened and ignorant manner if, through their own carelessness or misunderstanding of Scripture, they are unaware of God's truth.

Verse 19 contains ideas that we commonly want to apply to all nonbelievers: sensuality, impurity, lust, a loss of sensitivity. While these expressions accurately describe many of the unsaved, this is the end result of darkness, not necessarily the first result.

While not totally unknown in the Christian community, these vices are usually not embraced by believers with the enthusiasm they are by some who have abandoned any controlling effort by God and who prefer to take their chances with their eternal destinies.

It is important to note that Paul wanted to make a strong point. He said, "I . . . insist on it in the Lord" (v. 17) as he told the Ephesian believers that they were not to live as the Gentiles or unsaved people do.

The believers in Ephesus had obviously not abandoned all of the old ways of thinking and doing. They needed prodding and reminding about the new values and life-style believers should adopt. They were living no better than their non-Christian acquaintances.

Light and Dark Contrasted

Your students who have not experienced the dregs of sin in their short lives may have one of two possible views regarding their non-Christian friends: (1) they may look with self-righteous disgust upon those who do not know

the Savior; (2) they might actually envy them.

On one hand your students might say, "I thank God that I am not like the tax collectors and drunkards" (see Luke 18:11) rather than saying, "There but for the grace of God go I."

On the other hand, some nonbelievers seem to have everything going for them. They are popular and seemingly carefree. They do not appear to have the conflict that Christians have between doing what they want to do and doing what is right.

The writer of Psalm 73 experienced this struggle with envy of the nonbeliever. He described his perception that the wicked are carefree, escaping the burdens and problems common to humanity, having no struggles, constantly increasing in wealth. He contrasted this seemingly trouble-free life-style with his own attempts to stay clean and pure. He began to feel that living for God just wasn't worth it! But eventually he realized the apparent external blessings of the wicked were not all that real or lasting, and that ultimately these people would receive the judgment that was due them. He came to this realization when he "entered the sanctuary of God" (Psalm 73:17). As he remembered what God meant to him, he saw things in their correct perspective. He concluded, "But as for me, it is good to be near God. I have made the Sovereign Lord my refuge; I will tell of all your deeds" (v. 28).

Sinners are in the sad state described in Ephesians 4:17-19 and Psalm 73:18,19 on the inside; but on the outside many are successful, happy and busy enjoying the good things of this life without any apparent pangs of conscience. Since we don't see into their hearts, we might think they've got it made!

Just reading Ephesians 4:17-19 and Psalm 73:18,19 will not convince many junior highers that nonbelievers are often unhappy people. All around them they see popular, with-it people who don't care about God at all. So they naturally begin to ask themselves, "What's so great about being a Christian?"

Today's session will encourage your students to look inside their non-Christian peers and try to understand the darkness and needs which are really there. If you were once a non-Christian teenager, help your class by telling them what it was like and how you realized you needed Christ.

Another Contrast

And what about the contrast, the "truth that is in Jesus" (Ephesians 4:21)? It's the opposite of all the negatives listed in verses 17-19! Christ gives purpose instead of futility, understanding instead of darkness, union instead of separation, truth instead of ignorance, sensitivity instead of hardness, love instead of sensuality, cleanness instead of impurity.

Neither the futility of sin nor the light of Christ are things that just happen to us. Notice the phrases "hardening of their hearts" (v. 18) and "they have given themselves over" (v. 19). Notice how the Christian is to "put off" the old self (see v. 22) and "put on" the new self (see v. 24). We make the choice, with God's help, to walk in the light.

The Lord is pleased with the slightest bit of willingness to live in His light. Even if your junior highers still have nagging envies of the happy-go-lucky non-Christians in their school, the Lord will accept and work with even their smallest glimmer of willingness to live as His.

SESSION PLAN

BEFORE CLASS BEGINS: Photocopy the Fun Page (for use in the CONCLUSION). There is no Key worksheet or Teaching Resource page this time. The second step of the EXPLORATION requires a few pictures cut from a fashion magazine and construction paper. From these you are to make, before class, several "Mr. and Ms. Cool X-ray Machines" as described in that step.

Attention Grabber

ATTENTION GRABBER (2-3 minutes)

Draw an extremely simple maze on the chalkboard like the one shown below. Ask a volunteer to complete the maze—with eyes closed!

After the volunteer has finished and sat down say, **The maze was impossible to do because you were limited by having your eyes closed. The maze would have been very simple to do if you had your eyes open. Today we are going to look at the way many people are spiritually handicapped as they go through life, and how this handicap can lead to serious problems and even to destruction.**

ALTERNATE ATTENTION GRABBER (3-5 minutes)

If there was a time in your childhood or adolescence when you were highly envious of another's special toy or good fortune, describe it to your students. Describe how you felt, what you thought about the object of your desires, what you think about it now and any other pertinent thoughts.

If your students like to share, ask if any of them could relate a similar experience.

Explain, **The Bible passages we are about to look at talk about the evil life-style of the non-Christian and the problems a believer can run into if he or she starts to envy that life-style. Though some may feel envy for the apparent success of the wicked, we'll see just how bad off they really are.**

Bible Exploration

EXPLORATION (35-45 minutes)

Materials needed: Fashion magazine and construction paper for use as described in Step 2.

Step 1 (2-3 minutes): Read Ephesians 4:17-24 together. Explain any words that students don't understand. Explain that "Gentile" originally meant someone who was not a Jew, and therefore came to mean "a person without God" in some cases.

Step 2 (15-20 minutes): Before class, cut out a few pictures of handsome male and female models from a fashion magazine. The pictures should be large photos of the models' faces. The best pictures would be ones that the students would judge as being too good-looking, too phoney. Glue the faces to construction paper. Cut the paper and label it as shown below. You should make one of these for every group of three or four students.

MR. COOL AND THE X-RAY MACHINE

Assemble students into groups of three or four (girls and boys in separate groups) and give each group one of the "X-ray machines" (Mr. Cool for the boys, Ms. Cool for the girls). Say, **Imagine that the picture you have is of a "Mr. or Ms. Cool"—someone who thinks he or she has the world on a string, not at all interested in God. A person who thinks he or she is successful, popular, in.**

But what Mr. or Ms. Cool seems like, on the outside, isn't what he or she is really like on the inside. God's Word is like an X-ray that sees what's going on in the person's heart. Let's X-ray Mr. and Ms. Cool and find out what they are like in there.

Have students reread Ephesians 4:17-19. Tell them, **When you find something in Ephesians 4:17-19 that tells you what a person without God is really like, draw a picture of that characteristic inside Mr. or Ms. Cool's X-ray. For example, in verse 18 where it mentions a hard heart, you might draw a heart-shaped block of concrete. Darkness might be a burned-out light bulb. If you can't think of a picture or symbol, just write a word or phrase inside Mr. or Ms. Cool.**

When the groups have had time to work, regain their attention and have them display and talk about what they've done. If you like, tack the posters to the wall and let everyone come up for a closer look.

Step 3 (8-10 minutes): Have students continue working in their groups. Ask them to reread Ephesians 4:20-24. Say, **Suppose Mr. or Ms. Cool realizes that "cool is the rule of the fool." That is, he or she wants to change for the better. I want you to use Ephesians 4:20-24 to help you answer two questions.** Write the following questions on the chalkboard for groups to answer on scratch paper.

1. What should he or she do to change?

2. What benefits will he or she experience?

Discuss students' answers when they have finished. Notice again how Mr. and Ms. Cool's will (what they want to do) is involved in the change from darkness to light. But notice how it ultimately depends on "the truth that is in Jesus" (v. 21). Only as a person learns the truth in Jesus will he or she be motivated to change; then God can help him or her make that change (see vv. 23,24).

Step 4 (10-12 minutes): Turn to Psalm 73. Tell learners that this psalm was written by someone who felt jealous of sinners. He looked around and saw that sinners seemed to be happier and better off and had fewer problems than God's people! Then the Lord showed him the truth.

Read the following verses (or have volunteers read) and ask students to discuss these questions:

1. Verses 1-3: **What did the writer feel in verse 3? Why?**

2. Verses 4-6: **What are the things that the writer thought the wicked people enjoyed? Do you think this is really the way it is with wicked people?**

3. Verse 16: **What was the writer's feeling as he considered what he thought to be the advantages of being evil?**

4. Verses 17-19: **Why did the writer change his mind about the wicked? What does it mean to enter "the sanctuary of God"? How can we do that today? What new opinion of the wicked did the writer then have?**

5. Verses 23,24: **What advantages does a righteous person have over the wicked?**

6. Verse 28: **What two commitments has the writer made to God?**

Thank everyone for their contributions to the discussion. Say, **We've looked at some heavy thoughts in this session. Let's take a few moments to think about how they might apply to us personally.**

Conclusion and Decision

CONCLUSION (5-7 minutes)

Distribute the Fun Page take-home paper. Read the story and the letter from the editor while students follow along on their own copies. Ask your learners to take a few moments in silent prayer, to consider their commitments to God. You can close by leading a prayer that a student who wants to make a first time commitment to God could echo silently. Make yourself available to anyone who wishes to talk to you after class.

NOTES

Your students may wish to see this solution to the Fun Page game:

If you walk in spiritual darkness, it is hard to watch out for Satan's traps. If you walk in regular darkness, you will goosh cockroaches.

TOWN CRIER

Based on Luke 22:39—23:46

IN THE GARDEN OF GETHSEMANE, JUST BEFORE HE WAS ABOUT TO BE BETRAYED AND CONDEMNED TO CRUCIFIXION, JESUS KNELT DOWN AND BEGAN TO PRAY, SAYING, "FATHER, IF YOU ARE WILLING, TAKE THIS CUP FROM ME; YET NOT MY WILL, BUT YOURS BE DONE" (LUKE 22:42).

THIS DEATH WAS IN FULFILLMENT OF OLD TESTAMENT PROPHECIES AND JESUS' PROMISES. HE DIED FOR OUR SINS THAT YOU AND I MIGHT **LIVE FOREVER.**

HE KEPT HIS PROMISES!

HE WAS TORTURED AND CRUCIFIED.

BEING IN AGONY OVER THE COMING ORDEAL, HE WAS PRAYING FERVENTLY. IN THE DARKNESS, HIS SWEAT WAS LIKE DROPS OF BLOOD ON THE GROUND.

LETTER FROM THE EDITOR:

Does God keep His promises? You bet He does!

As we saw above, even in the face of the horrible ordeal of torture that Jesus Christ had to endure He kept every promise, word for word.

You and I—if you are a Christian—have been saved by His faithfulness to His promises.

In the everyday world we live in, it is sometimes easy to forget the debt we owe to God. We forget our Christianity, we begin to value unimportant things—things that non-Christians may hold so dear.

When I begin to do that, I remind myself of one thing: God has promised me many wonderful blessings and rewards for all eternity. And He's faithful. He'll keep His commitment to me.

That thought encourages me to keep my commitment to Him.

"So I tell you this, and insist on it in the Lord, that you must no longer live as the Gentiles do, in the futility of their thinking. They are darkened in their understanding and separated from the life of God." Ephesians 4:17,18

"If we claim to have fellowship with him yet walk in the darkness, we lie and do not live by the truth. But if we walk in the light, as he is in the light, we have fellowship with one another, and the blood of Jesus, his Son, purifies us from all sin." 1 John 1:6,7

God wants us to walk in His light rather than stumble about in the world's spiritual darkness. With that in mind, here's a code for you to decipher. The decoded message will teach you two important things about walking in darkness. Well, one of them is important anyway. You decide which.

Instructions: Reproduced here is the push-button face of a standard telephone. Use it to translate the number code. Because each numeral on the phone gives three letters, you'll need to decide which letters to use. Watch out for the second to last word in the code; it's a bit tough.

43 968 9255 46 77474 8825 3275 63377, 48
47 4273 86 92824 688
367 72826'7 87277.
43 968 9255 46
7348527 32756377,
968 9455 46674
262576222437.

"You were taught, with regard to your former way of life, to put off your old self, which is being corrupted by its deceitful desires; to be made new in the attitude of your minds; and to put on the new self, created to be like God in true righteousness and holiness."
Ephesians 4:22-24

DAILY THINKERS

Day 1 Read Ephesians 4:27. What are ways you could give the devil an opportunity? What are ways you can keep the devil away?

Day 2 Ephesians 4:28. List some ways you can share with those in need. (Hint: Money is not the only way you can share.)

Day 3 Ephesians 4:29. If you follow the instructions Paul gives in this verse, what effect will it have on those around you?

Day 4 Ephesians 4:30. What do you think causes the Holy Spirit to grieve?

Day 5 Ephesians 4:31. Underline the traits in this verse which you are to get rid of. Make a list of their opposites.

Day 6 Ephesians 4:32. Write this verse on a piece of paper and hang it where you will see it often. Try to memorize this verse.

THEME: The old self and the new self.

Session 8

BIBLE STUDY OUTLINE

Do the Object Lesson, then read Romans 6:1-14 to your students. Make the following remarks as time allows.

Introductory remarks: Throughout human history, people have enslaved other people, imprisoned enemies, tortured people, performed horrible "medical experiments" such as those at some Nazi prison camps, crucified, maimed and caged people. But no matter how inhumane the prison guards or how high the prison walls, no person on earth has ever been tortured or caged forever. Sooner or later, everyone is released from their earthly hardships. Even those subjected to lifelong prison terms eventually leave the prison. How? If by no other way, they are released by death.

Sin also enslaves and traps people. Sin will never willingly let a person go. But when a person dies to sin and comes alive to Christ, that person is freed from the power of sin. The death of the old nature is the way to freedom from sin. The passage we'll look at now talks about the death of the old self and our new life in Christ.

Verse 1: We all know that when we come to Christ His grace takes care of our sins. He forgives our sins; He died on the cross to destroy the power of sin over us. Paul asks, "Does that make it OK to keep on sinning?"

Verses 2-4: The answer, of course, is a resounding "No." In verse 3, Paul shows how baptism pictures a changed life. Going into the water was like being buried in a grave; coming out of the water was like coming out of the grave with a new life, just as Jesus did. Since we joined Jesus in death, now we are to join Him in a new, godly life. Unhappily, some Christians try to get their old sinful natures to come back to life, too! That is why Paul is writing about these things.

Verses 5-7: The whole point to this death of the old nature, Paul tells us, is that we are no longer slaves to sin. We are no longer part of the devil's family; we belong to God. We are now free to become the people God wants us to be.

Verses 8-10: Dying to Satan's control and being born into God's family happens the moment we become Christians. This new life is a fact for those of us who belong to God.

Verses 11-14: Because we have this new life, we are supposed to act like it. The whole point to Paul's argument is that the Christian is to stop behaving like a member of Satan's world and start living a good, moral life like a child of God. God has made us dead to sin; now we are supposed to act like it. We are not slaves of sin, we are servants of God.

Paul wants us to be free from sin. He has given us three steps to take: (1) realize we are dead to sin; (2) refuse to let sin reign over us; (3) turn our lives over to God for righteous service.

OBJECT LESSON: SYMBOL OF DEATH

Get your learners thinking about death by showing a picture of a graveyard, a wilted bouquet, a black arm band or some other symbol of death. **Ask, what does this symbol make you think of? What are some obvious signs of death?**

DISCUSSION QUESTIONS

1. **If God can forgive us for any sin, what are some reasons why it's important we still try very hard not to sin?**

2. **If both non-Christians and Christians sin, what do you think is the advantage of being a Christian and dead to sin?**

3. **Paul said that we are to realize we are dead to sin, refuse to let sin reign over us and turn our lives over to God as instruments of righteousness. What does the word "righteous" mean and what are some acts of righteousness that a Christian your age could do?**

Broom Games

BROOM BALANCE RELAY

Assemble two or more teams in single file behind a starting line. At a signal, the first player on each team moves as fast as possible to an object (such as a chair), circles it and comes back. The catch is that the player must balance a long broom on one hand. If a player drops a broom or touches it with his or her second hand, the player must start over at the starting line. If a player is having too much trouble with the broom, let him or her pass it off to the next player. Each team should have its own object to circle, unless you want to create extra chaos.

BALL SWEEP

Place two parallel lines of tape on the floor, 15 feet apart. (This game works best on a hard surface.) See the illustration for proper team positions.

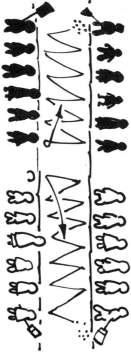

You need four brooms and several small, hard rubber balls. The balls should come in two colors, one color for each team (spray paint works well). The more balls, the better.

The object of the game is for team members to sweep the balls from one side of the playing field to the other, from teammate to teammate until all the balls have been swept from the very first team member to the very last. The first team to complete the task wins.

Give a broom to the first player on each team, the player at the end of a row. Place the proper colored balls at the feet of the players with the brooms. Also give a broom to each player's teammate standing opposite him or her. The first player will attempt to sweep the balls across the floor to his or her teammate who is also holding a broom. The first player must sweep all the balls completely across the opposite line; the first player's teammate must sweep them all together again, then sweep the balls back across the playing field to the third player (now holding the first player's broom). On it goes until all the players on one team have taken a turn to sweep the balls. The final player can sweep the balls back to the original starting point. On a hard surface such as concrete or linoleum, this is not an easy job—in the heat of competition, the balls seem to have minds of their own!

Rules to Live By SESSION 9

WHAT THE SESSION IS ABOUT
Marks of a growing Christian.

SCRIPTURE STUDIED
Ephesians 4:25-32

KEY PASSAGE
"Be kind and compassionate to one another, forgiving each other, just as in Christ God forgave you."
Ephesians 4:32

AIMS OF THE SESSION
During this session your learners will:

1. Contrast do's and don'ts in Ephesians 4:25-32 and think about the reasons for each of them;
2. Give an example of a practical way to demonstrate at least one of God's "do's";
3. Identify specific areas in their Christian lives in which they need to stop or start doing specific actions.

INSIGHTS FOR THE LEADER

If any Scripture seems to read like a list of rules, it's Ephesians 4:25-32. And it's all excellent spiritual advice. Don't lie. Don't sin. Don't give the devil an opportunity. Don't steal. Work with your hands. Keep your talk clean. Don't grieve the Holy Spirit. Get rid of bitterness. Be kind.

We can never earn God's forgiveness or favor by living a "good" life. This passage, therefore, is not a formula for "getting in good" with God. These are actions and attitudes that grow within the Christian as a result of having already received new life in Christ.

These do's and don'ts—and others in other parts of Scripture—are practical helps to guide Christ's people to live together in peace with each other and in a way that honors God. They are solid guidelines for the everyday lives of those who have already come to know His forgiveness, not the route to obtaining that forgiveness.

How New People Live
God's people have an enemy: the devil. He "prowls around like a roaring lion looking for someone to devour" (see 1 Peter 5:8). He looks for an opportunity, a "foothold" (Ephesians 4:27) where he can latch onto us and drag us down. Giving in to the sins mentioned in Ephesians 4:25-32 will open a door to Satan. Notice how the sins of lying, inappropriate anger, stealing, unwholesome talk and

bitterness seem especially designed to cause havoc in Christian relationships. Let's take a closer look at these problems.

1. Lying. Carelessness about the truth can drive a wedge between people. If you aren't sure that I will be honest, you won't trust me with important things in your life. If I'm careless about caring for and returning property I have borrowed, you won't want to lend me your favorite recording. If I break my promise to keep a secret, you won't tell me the hard struggle you are going through. Worst of all, if we as Christians lie, we will make it hard for people to believe what we say about our Lord. When people measure the integrity of our faith, they look at the worth of our words. If we make claims about everyday life that are not true, our claims about spiritual things will be suspect as well.

2. Inappropriate anger. We know that anger can be appropriate. We should be angry when people are mistreated or when God's ways are opposed or disobeyed. Jesus showed anger over these two types of situations (see Mark 3:5 and John 2:13-17). But much anger arises from more selfish motivations: things aren't going our way; we aren't getting what we want; someone is frustrating our desires. This kind of anger can come to us in a moment, without our really wanting it or seeking it out. This is the type of anger that Paul tells us to set aside before the end of the day.

NOTES

The longer we hold onto it, the worse the situation will get. A prompt reconciliation with the other person can prevent a lot of unhappiness. Most situations we get angry about are not really worth the problems caused by our anger.

3. Stealing. Christians have no business taking what does not belong to us. We are called to high standards of honesty and integrity.

4. Unwholesome talk. "Dirty jokes" and other unclean types of speech are not appropriate for Christians. Conversation that causes hearers to think wrong thoughts or to judge another person also comes under this category. So does the kind of kidding or cruel "cutting" that causes hard feelings or sadness in the victim. While God has nothing against good, clean fun and humor, sometimes teasing that is intended only to be fun between friends can turn ugly or be interpreted as an attack.

5. Grieving the Holy Spirit. We grieve Him when we disobey the Word and the known will of God (for example, by committing any of the sins discussed in this passage). We also grieve Him when we ignore God by neglecting our time with Him. Once we are believers, the Holy Spirit is in our lives permanently. When we grieve Him He does not go away from us. We have our choice: We can live out of harmony with a Holy Spirit who is grieved with us or we can live at peace with a Holy Spirit who is not grieved.

6. Bitterness. If we hold onto our anger and resentments long enough, they turn into bitterness. Christians should give no place to this type of emotion. The command in Ephesians 4:31 is "get rid of." It does not say, "if you feel like it." It implies, "do it anyway." Getting rid of bitterness takes an act of the will that must override our emotions. God knows the damage that bitterness can do in our lives and in our relationships with Him and others. Therefore, the sternness of this command is an expression of love and concern for our well-being.

On the Other Hand

Having looked at the "no-nos" of the Christian life, let's take a peek at some of the "yes-yeses."

1. Speak truthfully. This is more than the flip side of "no lying." Speaking the truth creates an atmosphere of trust and confidence that is essential among believers. A Christian's word is his or her bond!

2. Work in order to share with those in need. Interestingly, Paul does not say, "Steal no longer, but work in order to support yourself." He goes beyond that and says that the former thief must help people who are in need—the opposite of what he or she was doing as a thief. Besides, it's important to work in order to deserve what we achieve or receive. For example, if we study hard we deserve the good grades we receive on tests; if we get the answers from others we are simply stealing those grades.

3. Speech that builds others up. Helping each other grow up in Christ should be a primary goal for believers. We can encourage one another to trust the Lord and to be faithful in Bible study, prayer and other basic Christian practices. We can point out the strengths and gifts we see in one another that can be used for God's service. We can encourage those who are trying to serve the Lord but are having difficulty or seeing disappointing results.

4. Kindness and compassion. These two traits involve looking outward, not inward, at the needs of others rather than of self. They involve courtesy and a willingness to help meet the needs of other people. They are part of the character of the Lord Jesus, so the more we practice them the more we are like Him.

SESSION PLAN

BEFORE CLASS BEGINS: Photocopy the Key worksheet and the Fun Page take-home paper. The Fun Page is used in the ALTERNATE CONCLUSION. The third step of the EXPLORATION requires several sheets of poster board and assorted colors of marking pens.

Attention Grabber

ATTENTION GRABBER (5-7 minutes)

When students have been seated, distribute pencils and scratch paper. Say, **I want you to imagine that you own a mansion filled with expensive objects that a burglar would just love to steal. In fact, a thief sneaks up to a side of your house that has four windows. One window is covered with steel bars, like a prison window. Another window is guarded by two incredibly ferocious attack dogs. The third window is protected by a Howitzer cannon. The fourth window is open and unprotected.**

First of all, which window do you think the thug is going to try to enter? Why? Work individually or in pairs to draw a window, protected by whatever means you can think of other than bars, dogs and cannons.

Give the students a few minutes to work, then allow volunteers to show what they have done. Some may have come up with some pretty outlandish ideas!

Make a transition to the EXPLORATION by saying, **Today's Scripture tells us not to give any opportunity to the devil. Just as that open window is an opportunity to the thief, certain things we do give Satan an open window to get into our lives as Christians.**

ALTERNATE ATTENTION GRABBER (5-7 minutes)

Ask students to share some of the do's and don'ts of their family or household. Listen and try not to be judgmental if students are not enthusiastic about some of the regulations in their families. After students have shared several household rules, ask them to look at the issue from another perspective: **What do's and don'ts do you enforce for other family members? For example, do you insist that your brothers and sisters keep their hands off your tape collection?**

Sum up what students have said then say, **All families have some rules or do's and don'ts for their family members to live by. God's family has do's and don'ts as well. The big difference is that in our human families we must live with human limitations. We try to do what we hope or think is best even if it is not. God, on the other hand, knows what is best. His do's and don'ts are practical and right. Let's take a look at some of them.**

Bible Exploration

EXPLORATION (30-45 minutes)

Step 1 (10-15 minutes): Introduce this activity by saying, **We're going to take a look at some do's and don'ts in the Bible. As you do this study, remember that these are not ways to earn God's favor. Rather, they are the responses that we as Christians are to make to the new life that He has given us as a free gift.**

This step may be done in small groups or individually. Have learners work on the "Two Sides to It" activity on their Key worksheets. They will read the indicated Scripture and follow the instructions given.

As students work, move around the room to offer encouragement and help. Today's Scripture can seem depressing, especially to a junior higher who is having trouble with truthfulness, anger, stealing or unwholesome talk. Be encouraging to your learners. It is possible to show them total acceptance even as you're being honest regarding what the Scripture says about sin.

Step 2 (10-15 minutes): Discuss your learners' answers to "Two Sides to It." Sample answers are shown below. Be sure to expand upon the short answers in your discussion.

For those verses that don't cover all three of the categories ("DO," "DON'T," and "WHY"), have students suggest their own ideas during the discussion. For example, students can probably think of several reasons why a Christian should not give the devil a foothold (Ephesians 4:27).

Verse 25:
   DO: Stop lying and start telling the truth.
   WHY: We belong to God's family.

Verse 26:
   DON'T: Let anger lead you to sin or hold a grudge.

Verse 27:
   DON'T: Give the devil an open window.

Verse 28:
   DON'T: Steal.
   DO: Work.
   WHY: To have something to share with the needy.

Verse 29:
   DON'T: Criticize others or swear.
   DO: Say good, helpful things.
   WHY: To build up and encourage others.

Verse 30:
   DON'T: Make the Holy Spirit sad.

Verse 31:
   DO: Get rid of bitterness, rage, anger, brawling, slander and malice.

Verse 32:
   DO: Be kind, compassionate and forgiving.
   WHY: Because Jesus forgave us.

Step 3 (12-15 minutes): Guide students into groups of two to four. Distribute two pieces of poster board and assorted colors of marking pens to each group. Explain, **You are going to make two old-fashioned "Wanted" posters. In fact, you are going to make one "Wanted" poster and one "Not Wanted" poster. On the "Not Wanted" poster, draw a picture of a bad-looking dude (or dudette) and list all the "don'ts" from Ephesians 4:25-32. These are the things that your criminal is guilty of. Also, make up at least one specific way in which this criminal actually did something wrong. For example,**

Ephesians 4:26 says, "Do not let the sun go down while you are still angry." You could write that the criminal tore up all his bed sheets because his little sister broke his bicycle. You can write some funny situations, but they should be something that a typical junior higher might do in real life.

On the other poster, the "Wanted" poster, draw a happy-looking person and list all the do's from Ephesians 4:25-32. These are the things your good person has done, the reasons he or she is *really* wanted. Make up and write on this poster at least one specific situation in which this person lived up to the Ephesians passage. Again, this should be something a junior high Christian can do in real life.

You may want to draw a sample poster on the chalkboard to give everyone an idea of what they should be developing. Walk from group to group to make sure everyone stays on track. When the posters are complete, allow students to show what they have done and read the situations they have written. Discuss how the situations relate to the daily lives of young people; add any insights needed.

Say, **You have demonstrated that you understand many of the traits that should be part of the lives of Christians. The problem is that many times we don't live up to the standards we believe and we don't follow the rules we endorse. Let's take a few moments to see how our lives relate to what we say.**

Conclusion and Decision

CONCLUSION (5-10 minutes)

Ask learners to turn to the "Squares and Circles" activity on the Key worksheet. Explain, **Scan Ephesians 4:25-32 in your Bibles, then follow the instructions on the Key worksheet to mark your response to some of the key ideas in the passage.**

You might want to share your own "squares" and "circles" as an example to your students that adults, too, need help from the Lord in their behavior as Christians.

Close with prayer.

Distribute the Fun Page take-home paper.

ALTERNATE CONCLUSION (5-7 minutes)

Distribute the Fun Page take-home paper. Ask students to individually and privately work the "How Do U-Rate?" game.

Then review the remarks at the end of the game, emphasizing that all people are sinners and explaining the two Bible verses noted.

Close in prayer.

TWO SIDES TO IT

Read Ephesians 4:25-32. The left side of this chart lists all those verses. Every verse that tells something you should DO, write what it says under "DO" in the proper space on the chart. Every verse that tells something you should NOT DO, write what it says under "DON'T." If a verse tells you WHY you should do or not do something, write the reason under "WHY," on the chart. Most verses don't have all three things.

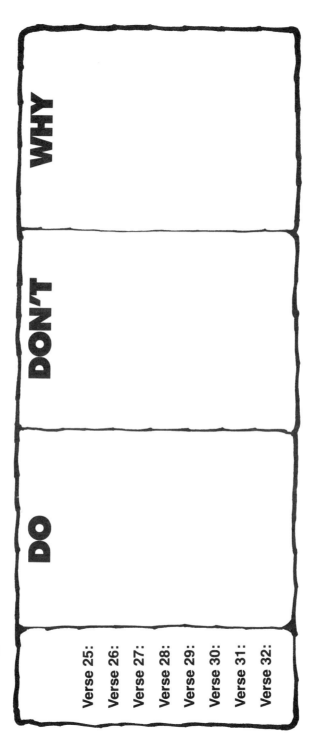

Verse	DO	DON'T	WHY
Verse 25:			
Verse 26:			
Verse 27:			
Verse 28:			
Verse 29:			
Verse 30:			
Verse 31:			
Verse 32:			

"Be kind and compassionate to one another, forgiving each other, just as in Christ God forgave you." Ephesians 4:32

SQUARES AND CIRCLES

CIRCLE any word or phrase that speaks of an area where you need to improve.

PUT A SQUARE AROUND any word or phrase that speaks of something that God has helped you with.

TELLING THE TRUTH   COMPASSION   KINDNESS   NOT STEALING   DOING USEFUL THINGS

HONESTY   BUILDING PEOPLE UP WITH WHAT I SAY   SHARING WITH PEOPLE IN NEED

FORGIVING   WORKING   NOT LETTING THE SUN GO DOWN ON ANGER

CARING FOR OTHERS

TOWN CRIER

"Be kind and compassionate to one another, forgiving each other, just as in Christ God forgave you." Ephesians 4:32

SPECIAL TOWN CRIER REPORT ON THE NINE COMMANDMENTS!

By staff star ace reporters Typo and Pifont
Based on Ephesians 4:24-32

The city of Ephesus—The world-famous nine commandments which God carved in stone and gave to Moses were examined in careful detail today by these reporters. In numerical order, the commandments are:

1. Put on the new self (In other words, be like Jesus Christ.)
2. Lay aside lies and falsehoods. Tell the truth.
3. Be angry, yet do not sin. Don't let the sun go down on your anger.
4. Don't give the devil an opportunity. (Especially with anger.)
5. Don't steal. Instead, work to earn a living and generously share with those in need.
6. Don't use foul or unwholesome speech. Say good things.
7. Do not grieve the Holy Spirit.
8. Stay away from bitterness, rage, anger, brawling, slander and malice.
9. Be kind, compassionate and forgiving.

Have you ever sinned? Of course you have! In fact, there's a very good chance you've broken EVERY ONE of the nine commandments mentioned in the *Town Crier* story!

If you doubt that, try filling out this chart we call

HOW DO U-RATE?

Instructions: The U-Rate chart lists nine ways a person could break the commandments of Ephesians 4:24-32. (The actual commands from Ephesians are in parentheses.) There are spaces for you to fill in with points. For example, if you've never lied about your homework, write zero points in the proper space. If you've lied about it just once or twice, put five points. If you lie a lot, put ten points. When finished, add up your points and compare to the U-Rate Score Card.

☐ Have you ever left the house knowing you were supposed to do chores first? (Put on the new self.)

☐ Have you ever lied about doing your homework? (Speak truthfully.)

☐ Have you ever gone to bed really angry at someone? (Don't let the sun go down on your anger.)

☐ Have you ever said anything in anger that hurt another's feelings? (Don't give the devil an opportunity.)

☐ Have you ever eaten something from the refrigerator you knew someone else was saving? (Don't steal.)

☐ Has your mouth ever uttered bad language? (No unwholesome talk.)

☐ Have you ever sinned? (Don't grieve the Holy Spirit.)

☐ Have you ever gossiped about someone? (Don't slander.)

☐ Have you ever held a grudge? (Forgive others.)

U-Rate Score Card

0 points: Hard to believe!
5-25 points: Sinner.
30-50 points: Sinner.
55-95 points: Sinner.

It's impossible to honestly get zero points; we all do wrong things every day. The bad news is, "Whoever keeps the whole law and yet stumbles at just one point is guilty of breaking all of it" (James 2:10). In other words, we are all sinners, even the best of us. The good news is, "If we confess our sins, he is faithful and just and will forgive us our sins and purify us from all unrighteousness" (1 John 1:9). Take your sins to God. He will forgive you and clean you up again!

DAILY THINKERS

Day 1   Read Ephesians 5:1,2. How did Christ show His love to you? What are some ways you can show your love to others?

Day 2   Ephesians 5:3. What three types of conduct does Paul call improper for Christians in this verse?

Day 3   Ephesians 5:4. What would you do if someone told you a dirty joke?

Day 4   Ephesians 5:5. Why does Paul call a greedy person an idolater? (See Exodus 20:3,4.) Do you place anything in your life before God?

Day 5   Ephesians 5:6,7. What might someone say to try to convince you to do something God would not like? What should you do?

Day 6   Ephesians 5:8,9. Underline the words which describe the fruit of the light. What person is often called "the light" in the Bible? (See John 1:4-7.)

THEME: A few rules to live by.

Session 9

BIBLE STUDY OUTLINE

Start off with the "If, Then" game, then read Philippians 4:4-9 to your students. Make the following remarks as time allows.

Verse 4: To rejoice means to be full of joy or to be exhilarated with pleasant sensations. While Paul does not state a particular reason why he wants his readers to rejoice, it's safe to assume he wanted them to be delighted by the wonderful things God had done for them. True Christian joy has its source in God, which means it's not ruined when outside circumstances turn bad. That's why Christians can "rejoice always."

What happens when a person rejoices in the Lord? His or her attitude is bright and cheerful; it's impossible to be sad or depressed if you are joyful!

Verses 5-7: In this context, the word gentleness means Christian love and consideration for others. This is another rule to live by, a habit to develop.

The next great event in God's plan is the return of Jesus Christ in power and victory. Because His return is sure, we needn't worry about anything. Worry is a lack of faith in God's ability to care for us. Instead, we are to take our cares to Him in thankful prayer. If we believe God answers prayer, then God's peace will fill our hearts and minds.

Verse 8: Saturate your mind with the fine things of God. Whatever fills the mind determines a person's behavior and feelings. If our minds are healthy, then our lives will be healthy too.

Verse 9: If you practice these rules to live the Christian life by, then God will be at your side.

To sum up: If we rejoice, show consideration, trust God in prayer, set our minds on the fine things of God and obey God's rules, then God's peace will fill us and we won't need to worry about things.

SILLY GAME: "IF, THEN"

To help your students grasp the truth that there are benefits for those who obey God's rules, let them play this game called "If, Then."

Each student needs two cards or sheets of paper of different colors. The student makes up an "if" statement and writes it on one card (such as, "If I eat chicken . . . "). On the other card he or she writes the logical "then" statement (" . . . then I break out in hives"). Be sure all the "if" statements go on one color of paper and all the "then" statements go on the other color of paper.

Collect and shuffle the cards in two stacks according to color. Draw an "if" card and read it. Draw a "then" card and read it. The random combinations will be silly, funny or downright impossible. Don't read any cards of questionable taste.

Point out that every "if" has a "then" in life, just like this game. Say, **Though these were silly or impossible ideas, it is true that if we obey God's rules and advice, then we will enjoy the benefits of our actions. Let's look at some things He tells us to do.**

DISCUSSION QUESTIONS

1. **What are some of the things God does for us that should fill us with joy?**

2. **Quite a few Christians would probably have to admit they are not always rejoicing in the Lord. What might be some things that prevent rejoicing?**

3. **What are some good things that might happen if we show consideration to those around us?**

Fun Stuff for a Picnic

PANIC PICNIC

Form two teams. Everyone holds hands in a circle, the two teams alternating around the circle. The circle of people should surround a small circle marked on the ground (with a loop of rope, for example). The object of the game is for each person to try to force the people whose hands he or she is holding to cross the line. Anyone forced to do so is out of the game. Continue playing until all players remaining are on the same team. Play several rounds, each time giving a point for each player who remains in the game. The final total determines the winning team.

PICNIC PYRAMID

An oldie: Two teams compete to see who can form the biggest human pyramid. Take it slow and easy.

HELLO, JELLO

If you're making a big batch of Jello for the picnic, make a second big batch. Spoon the finished Jello into shallow bowls or baking pans, one per contestant. Insert marbles into the Jello. Contestants can use only their mouths to remove the marbles. First player to remove all the marbles from his or her Jello wins. Whip cream on the Jello adds a nice touch.

Opportunities

WHAT THE SESSION IS ABOUT

We should be looking for and using the opportunities God has given to us to grow in and share our faith.

SCRIPTURE STUDIED

Matthew 8:28-34; Mark 4:21-25; 10:46-52

KEY PASSAGE

"Be very careful, then, how you live—not as unwise but as wise, making the most of every opportunity, because the days are evil." Ephesians 5:15,16

AIMS OF THE SESSION

During this session your learners will:

1. Examine opportunities that several biblical characters had and how they responded to them;
2. List ways Christians can take advantage of the opportunities God gives them;
3. Determine at least one area of their lives to examine for opportunities for growth and sharing their faith.

INSIGHTS FOR THE LEADER

Ephesians 5:15,16 says, "Be careful, then, how you live—not as unwise but as wise, making the most of every opportunity, because the days are evil."

First, Paul tells us *what* to do: Be careful how we lead our lives. That is, we are to live like God tells us to in the Bible. All of your students would accept that statement as obvious—yet so many fail to put it into practice on a daily basis! That is why we teach them, trusting God to help them blossom into mature, godly disciples.

Paul then tells us *how* to live carefully: With wisdom, grabbing the opportunities God presents. Christian wisdom is to take every opportunity to lead a godly life. There are 24 hours of opportunities in every day; the wise person makes the most of them by living as the Bible says, but the fool does no such thing.

Finally, Paul tells us *why* we should live carefully: The days are evil. We live in an environment of evil. All of us are immersed in a flood of evil, rushing at us from all sides. Anyone who does not wisely grab opportunities to live according to God's wishes is like a drowning fool refusing to grasp for a nearby safety ring. Not to live carefully and wisely is to be swamped by the world's evil. A Christian who surrenders to evil is a Christian whose life will be shattered and of little positive spiritual consequence in this world.

Our chief focus in this session is Paul's admonition to make the most of our opportunities. In order to help students more fully understand the idea of making the most of every opportunity, the session will also guide them in examining three additional Scriptures.

Opportunities Gained and Lost

Mark 4:21-25 includes the record of Jesus saying, "Do you bring in a lamp to put it under a bowl or a bed? Instead, don't you put it on its stand?" (v. 21). Having a functional lamp in an otherwise dark room gives us an opportunity to continue doing the productive and enjoyable things we have done during daylight hours. A portable lamp or flashlight gives us an opportunity to move around outside at night without stumbling over some unseen obstacle or falling down.

Jesus used this saying to illustrate the obvious point that light is to be used for the purpose for which it was designed. Light in this case represents our new spiritual nature. Christians are to be lights in the world, shining to help people find the truth about God. If we hide ourselves, we are not making the most of the opportunities God gives us to share.

Mark 10:46-52 tells the story of a blind man named Bartimaeus who made the most of an opportunity that came to him one day. Jesus came by the place Bartimaeus was sitting. Bartimaeus shouted over the noise of the crowds and over the objections of those

NOTES

around him until Jesus stopped to talk to him. He asked for his sight to be restored and Jesus did what he wanted. This was a man who wasn't going to let opportunity pass him by! He had to take a risk because the people around him didn't like his shouting like that. He risked making a spectacle of himself. He risked the anger of people upon whose alms he depended. He risked disappointment. But his courage was repaid with the ability to see. He could see the dusty road at his feet and the crowds that surrounded him. Best of all, he could look upon the face of the One who had healed him.

Matthew 8:28-34 tells of the time Jesus cast evil spirits out of two men in an area populated by people called the Gadarenes. The spirits begged to be allowed to enter a herd of pigs. Jesus granted permission, and the pigs rushed into the lake and drowned. The people tending the pigs ran to the nearby town and reported this event. The whole town went out to meet Jesus and to plead with Him to leave their area. They really missed an opportunity! They could have

asked Him to heal their sick and cast out more evil spirits. They could have listened to His teaching about the Father. They could have found light and love and eternal life—and a friend! Instead, frightened at something they didn't quite understand, and concerned about the economic disaster that might result from having Him around (what if all the animals in town went and drowned themselves?), they simply pushed Him away.

Many people have rejected Christ for the same kinds of reasons. They don't want Him to meddle in their affairs; they don't want the economy of their lives disrupted, so they pass up the chance to gain eternal life and to have the living God come into their presence. Quite an opportunity to throw away!

Encourage your students to follow the example of Bartimaeus by taking advantage of the opportunity to receive the help Jesus can give them. Encourage them to avoid the example of the Gadarene people who chased Him away rather than exploring something heretofore unknown to them.

SESSION PLAN

BEFORE CLASS BEGINS: Photocopy the Fun Page. There is no Key worksheet this time. The Teaching Resource page does not need to be copied unless you plan to have more than eight small groups during class. Cut apart the cards on the page, keeping the "Friend in Need" cards separate from the "Friend Indeed" cards. Both sets of cards are used in the third step of the EXPLORATION. The ATTENTION GRABBER calls for an inexpensive prize. Index cards are needed for the CONCLUSION.

Attention Grabber

ATTENTION GRABBER (6-8 minutes)

Materials needed: Inexpensive prize such as a gift certificate to an ice cream parlor.

Before class write the following on the chalkboard: "Win a free (name of prize)! Be the first one to decode this message and it's yours."

When students have arrived, write the letters found in the expression "opportunity knocks"—scrambling the order of the letters. Depending on the ability level of your class, you may wish to indicate that there are two words, keeping the letters for each one separate; or you may wish to scramble all the letters together.

Award the prize to the first student who correctly figures out the expression.

Tell your learners, **Today we are going to look at some Scripture passages that talk about making the best possible use of the time and opportunities that God has given us. Let's see what God's Word has to say.**

Bible Exploration

EXPLORATION (30-40 minutes)

Step 1 (3-5 minutes): Read Ephesians 5:15,16 to your class. Use the first part of the INSIGHTS FOR THE LEADER to help you explain the passage to your students.

Step 2 (12-15 minutes): Read the following passages to your students then lead a class discussion using the following questions.

Mark 4:21-25
1. **What are the two things one might do with a lamp?**
2. **What does this mean to a Christian teenager today?**

Mark 10:46-52
1. **What was "Bart's" opportunity?**
2. **Was it an easy chance to take? Why or why not?**
3. **Why do you think he was successful?**

Matthew 8:28-34
1. **Who passed up a great opportunity?**
2. **Why did they do so?**
3. **Why do people pass up coming to Christ today?**

Use material as needed from the INSIGHTS FOR THE LEADER to help learners realize that

Bartimaeus made the most of his opportunity to receive help from Jesus, while the Gadarenes passed up the same sort of opportunity. The discussion of the lamp shows us that we are to fulfill our intended purpose and take advantage of opportunities to share the light of Jesus Christ with those around us.

Step 3 (15-20 minutes): Assemble students into groups of two or three students each. To each group give scratch paper, one "Friend in Need" card and one "Friend Indeed" card from the Teaching Resource page. (Or you can let students draw the cards from two containers.)

Tell students, **In the Scripture passages we discussed, we saw an example of an opportunity that was missed and one that was taken advantage of with great results. Now let's consider some of the natural opportunities that we have to know more about Jesus and share Him with others.**

Look at the cards you've received. The "Friend in Need" cards each refer to a problem situation such as, "Craig feels lousy because his only Christian friend just moved away." The "Friend Indeed" cards each contain an area in which the average junior high Christian has an opportunity to do something constructive for another person.

NOTES

For example, one "Friend Indeed" card says, "You have extra spending money." How could a Christian use his or her money to help Craig?

Work together in your groups to come up with some creative ways a Christian your age could be a friend indeed to a friend in need. Your list should contain spiritually meaningful things a Christian could do for a person in need. For example, if you had extra spending money, you might treat Craig to a phone call to his Christian friend.

Encourage your students to list as many ideas as they can in about 10 or 12 minutes. Some groups may feel that their two cards don't fit together; let them draw new cards or trade a card with another group. Also, if you have time, you might have groups exchange cards every couple of minutes.

After students have had time to work, regain their attention and ask them to share some of the things they have listed. Add a few ideas of your own if students have missed some.

Say, **You have thought of some good ways people can use the many opportunities that God has given to His children. These opportunities are of no value if we merely recognize them without acting on them. Let's take a moment to consider what we can do in at least one of these areas—something we could do today or this week.**

Conclusion and Decision

CONCLUSION (5-7 minutes)

Materials needed: Blank index cards, felt pens.

Tell students, **You're going to make a "Clock Thought" based on what we have studied today. Take the index card I give you and either rewrite a portion of the passage in Ephesians 5:15,16 or create your own slogan based on that passage. Be sure to include some reference to an opportunity you're going to seize this week—either for your own spiritual growth, or for sharing God's love with another. (You may use one of the opportunities we just discussed.) You can take your card home and attach it to or set it on your clock in your room to remind you to make the most of every day for the glory of God, the benefit of others and your own spiritual growth.**

Allow students time to work. Ask a few volunteers to share their slogans.

Close in prayer.

Distribute the Fun Page take-home paper.

FRIEND IN NEED	FRIEND IN NEED	FRIEND INDEED
Craig feels lousy because his only Christian friend just moved away.	Heather thinks that God hates her.	You have extra spending money.
FRIEND IN NEED	FRIEND IN NEED	FRIEND INDEED
Jessica knows nothing about God or Jesus.	James has just gotten a job that will keep him away from Bible study meetings.	Your youth minister knows a lot about the Bible.
FRIEND IN NEED		FRIEND INDEED
Taylor's atheist teacher ridicules his faith.		As a Christian, you enjoy the privilege of prayer.
FRIEND IN NEED		FRIEND INDEED
It's obvious Dawn drinks before school.		There's a terrific, special youth group event coming up this week.
FRIEND IN NEED	FRIEND INDEED	FRIEND INDEED
Nathan lies—even to his friends.	You see this person sitting alone in the cafeteria.	Something just like this problem once happened to you and God helped you work it out.
FRIEND IN NEED	FRIEND INDEED	FRIEND INDEED
Kelly foolishly struggles to be popular by gossiping.	Your Bible teacher just covered this topic last night.	You can sit next to this person on the bus home from school.

TOWN CRIER

JONAH SURVIVES IN FISH STOMACH!

"Be very careful, then, how you live—not as unwise but as wise, making the most of every opportunity, because the days are evil." Ephesians 5:15,16

By super star reporter Typo
Based on Jonah 1:1-3; 3:1-3

Nineveh—A strange but incredibly true incident rocked the citizens of this great city today. A man named Jonah, who had been swallowed by a huge fish three days ago, was vomited upon the beach early this morning!

"It was awful," coughed eyewitnesses. "We were fishing on the beach when all of a sudden this giant fish barfs all this gunk all over the place. I mean, there were half-digested fish guts, slimy seaweed, gross-looking who-knows-whats.

"And then, out of this pile of rotting garbage climbs a MAN! We couldn't believe it. And what a mess! His hair had been digested off, his skin looked like a sunburned prune and . . . ."

Well, this reporter had heard enough. Holding my queasy stomach, I found the man himself, Jonah. He had washed himself and put on a fresh set of clothes. Yet a little stench still lingered. I covered my nose.

"I was running from God," Jonah told me. "He

commanded me to come to Nineveh and preach to the citizens. No way!"

"Why not?" I asked.

"Are you kidding? The Ninevites are mean and crazy! Why, did you know that when they invade an enemy city, they kill all the men and pile the skulls in the city square?" I didn't know. I wish I still didn't.

"While I was in the fish, I decided that I will do what God wants me to. But, wow! I hope those evil Ninevites don't do horrible, rotten things to me! Imagine!" I didn't want to imagine.

Suddenly a voice came down from heaven saying, "Go to the great city of Nineveh and proclaim to it the message I give you."

"Well, looks like I'd better go. It's a suicide mission." I decided I wouldn't tag along.

WELL, THE NINEVITES REPENTED. PEOPLE WERE SAVED. JONAH HAD TRIED TO RUN FROM GOD, BUT WHEN HE TURNED AROUND AND OBEYED, GREAT THINGS HAPPENED.

IF YOU ARE RUNNING FROM GOD—OR JUST TRYING TO IGNORE HIM— YOU ARE MISSING A WONDERFUL OPPORTUNITY TO EXPERIENCE THE LOVE AND PRESENCE OF GOD IN YOUR LIFE.

CLIMB OUT OF THE FISH'S STOMACH AND LET GOD USE YOU!

"Be very careful, then, how you live—not as unwise but as wise, making the most of every opportunity, because the days are evil." Ephesians 5:15,16

Have you ever walked into math class only to realize that you totally forgot about the major test the class is about to take? You didn't study and now you're going to die! Or have you ever said or done something so totally dumb, so ridiculously idiotic, that you've fouled up your life and you'll regret it forever?

Then maybe you've wished you could travel back in time and relive the event, or avoid the stupid thing you said or did.

Well, wish no longer. Try the

ACME TIME-TRAVEL MACHINE!

The secret of time travel is to travel faster than the speed of light. That's how Superman does it, you know.

Converted car springs, triggered to release at precisely the instant leg muscles receive 45,000,000—volt "stimulation," propel subject straight up at incredible, hyper-light speeds.

Hand-held air foils help subject control trajectory for the split second he or she remains in earth's atmosphere. After that, subject is on his or her own. Optional air supply for breathing in space available at extra cost.

Thick leather girdle nearly stops heart, lungs and stomach from being turned to mush in the soles of subject's feet due to high acceleration.

Diesel generator supplies gently to the ground in the event subject actually returns to earth. Parachute warranty available at extra cost.

Parachute wafts subject gently to the ground in the event subject actually returns to earth. Parachute warranty available at extra cost.

Headgear protects subject from impact with overhead objects such as ceilings, airplanes and the planet Saturn.

Since it is impossible to determine exactly how far back in time subject will travel, Acme includes this easy-to-understand dictionary of all known languages, past and present, allowing subject to read calendars to determine year and day. Also included are sign language symbols to use with cavemen, and tips on how to avoid death by dinosaur.

Mechanical hands exert tremendous pumping pressure on ankles to squeeze blood back up into subject's body.

Earplugs almost prevent damage to sensitive ear parts as subject goes screaming skyward.

Steel shoelaces to prevent shoes from being blasted off.

Maybe Jonah wished he could go back in time to avoid the three-day fish trip. And maybe there are things in your life that you wish you could go back in time and change.

It's impossible. Even the strange people at Acme can't time-travel.

But if you follow the advice of Ephesians 5:16—to make the most of the time you have each day—then you will be pleasing God and you'll be enjoying the time of your life.

■ DAILY THINKERS ■

Day 1 Read Ephesians 5:10. Make a list of the things you do which would please the Lord. Now make a list of the things you do which would displease the Lord. Which list is longer?

Day 2 Ephesians 5:13,14. Can you hide your conduct from God? How should this affect your actions?

Day 3 Ephesians 5:15,16. What are some opportunities you have to serve God in your daily life?

Day 4 Ephesians 5:18. What kinds of sin can getting drunk lead to? What has God given us instead of drunkenness?

Day 5 Ephesians 5:19,20. Write a verse thanking the Lord for specific things He has done for you. Do you feel thanks in your heart for these things? What is the difference between feeling thanks in your heart and thinking thanks with your mind?

Day 6 Ephesians 5:21. How is your walk as a Christian visible to your family, your friends, your classmates?

Session 10

THEME: Missed opportunities to turn to God.

BIBLE STUDY OUTLINE

Read Matthew 11:20-24 to your students. Make the following remarks as time allows.

Introductory remarks: Ephesians 5:15,16 tells us, "Be very careful, then, how you live—not as unwise but as wise, making the most of every opportunity, because the days are evil." What happens when a person does *not* make the most of every opportunity? Let's look at Matthew 11:20-24 to learn about some people who had the opportunity to see Jesus firsthand, yet rejected Him.

Verse 20: Why did Jesus denounce the cities? Because the people in those cities did not repent, even though they had seen the power of Jesus' works and heard the power of His words. Jesus did not come to entertain us. He demands that we turn our lives over to Him.

Verse 21: Korazin and Bethsaida were two of the many cities to which Jesus traveled. There He performed miracles and spoke to the people. Tyre and Sidon were farther north—Gentile cities to which Jesus never went. If they had seen Jesus, the people there would have humbled themselves and turned to God.

Verse 22: Judgment is coming to the people of those cities, as it comes for all people everywhere. For the people who saw Jesus but rejected him, judgment will be more terrible than for those who never saw Him.

Verses 23,24: Capernaum was Jesus' headquarters for much of His ministry. The people there had many opportunities to see and hear Jesus. That is why their condemnation was so much greater—even greater than Sodom, the capital of evil in the Old Testament days. The men of Sodom were practicing homosexuals. Yet if they had seen the power of Jesus, they would have repented. Not Capernaum. Capernaum's people therefore face a harsher judgment.

We might ask ourselves, "How can anyone see the miracles and hear the truth direct from the Son of God and still reject Him? How could they be so stupid?" Yet today, perhaps in this room, there are those who know all about Jesus, what He did and what He taught, but still they will not commit themselves fully to God. It's a scary thing to miss the opportunity to live for Jesus. Judgment is coming and it won't be fun for those who reject Jesus. (Do the Object Lesson.)

OBJECT LESSON: GLOBE

Show your listeners a globe or a picture of the earth. Say, **Science tells us that if we leave the earth in a starship traveling at or near the speed of light, time will begin to change. To someone on the ship, ship time will seem to stay the same, while time on earth will seem to accelerate. According to the theory of relativity, after a couple of years in space, traveling at the speed of light, we would return to earth two years older. But the people we left behind would be long gone, dead of old age! Time would have run out for them.**

Time is running out for everybody. God has given us all 24 hours a day. But our days are numbered. Make the most of every opportunity God gives you to live for Him. If you haven't become a Christian, you should seriously consider the benefits and consequences of doing so. If you are a Christian, live fully for Him every hour. Time is quickly running out. God will hold each of us accountable for the time we have been given.

DISCUSSION QUESTIONS

1. **Why do you suppose the people Jesus denounced didn't repent even though they had seen the miracles and heard the truth? What are some reasons people still reject Him today?**

2. **What does it mean to repent? What do we repent from? Why does God want us to repent?**

3. **What are some ways we can make "the most of every opportunity" (Ephesians 5:16)?**

GAMES & THINGS

Here is a good game to help everyone get to know each other a bit better. Photocopy the chart below, enough for everyone to have a copy. You, the leader of the game, read the top left square ("Lots of freckles"). Anyone who has lots of freckles checks off the box. Read the next box and allow players to check it off if they qualify. Do this for all the boxes. Make it clear that no player is to jump ahead to boxes you haven't read yet. As soon as a player has five squares in a row—horizontal, vertical or diagonal—he or she jumps up and yells "bingo." Let the crowd judge to see if the person does qualify (that he or she does have lots of freckles and so forth). Keep reading the boxes as time permits to have other finishers.

Lots of freckles.	Four or more kids in your family.	Never been to our meetings before.	Blond hair.	Wearing deodorant.
Ambidextrous. (If you don't know what it is, you ain't it.)	Wearing blue clothing.	Is not wearing socks.	Boy.	Black hair.
Brown hair.	Blue eyes.	Has the number 7 in phone number.	Under five feet tall.	Left-handed.
More than five letters in middle name.	Plays musical instrument.	Double-jointed thumbs.	Has been out of the country.	Girl.
Over five feet tall.	Green eyes.	Right-handed.	First name has two syllables.	Brown eyes.

Parents

WHAT THE SESSION IS ABOUT
Child-parent relationships in Christ.

SCRIPTURE STUDIED
Ephesians 6:1-4

KEY PASSAGE
"Children, obey your parents in the Lord, for this is right." Ephesians 6:1

AIMS OF THE SESSION
During this session your learners will:
1. Play a game based on Ephesians 6:1-4;
2. Discuss ways to improve their relationships with parents;
3. Write a letter to their parents to help build good relationships with them.

INSIGHTS FOR THE LEADER

Here is a classic "hot button" with young teenagers: Obedience and respect for parents! But it is commanded in the Bible and it's an important topic for junior highers. Your students will benefit greatly by understanding the mutual family responsibilities expressed in Ephesians 6:1-4. Accept the challenge of this lesson, praying that the Lord will open your students' hearts and that there will be an attentive spirit in the class.

The Christian Family
Today's Scripture is part of a larger passage that began in verse 21 of Ephesians, chapter 5. Paul presents a remarkable view of a family unit where each individual recognizes Christ as the Head and therefore honors Christ by submitting to other family members. The principle of mutual respect and caring between husband and wife sets the stage for similar honor and affection between parents and children. Your teenagers need to view verses 1-3 of chapter 6 not as an adult-level conspiracy in which God and parents seek to control children's lives, but as part of the complete context of guidelines for the Christian life given in chapters 4-6.

Ephesians 6 begins with the instruction "Children, obey your parents in the Lord, for this is right" (v. 1). It is a rather blunt directive: obey. The only justification or explanation given is that "this is right." It does not say, "for

this is fun" nor "for this is easy," but, "for this is right." That's the same justification all Christians have for obeying their heavenly Father—it is right to do so. We aren't told to obey Him when we feel like it or when it's easy, but because it is right to obey.

Yet this Scripture goes on to say more. Quoting the fifth commandment (see Deuteronomy 5:16; Exodus 20:12), verse 2 of Ephesians 6 instructs children to honor their parents. It includes a promise: "That it may go well with you and that you may enjoy long life on the earth" (v. 3). Society is more stable, life is better and the world runs more smoothly when children and parents live in harmony. God has arranged things that way, and He has promised a blessing when parents are honored by their children.

The action of honoring is one that your students may need to think about with creativity. Many junior highers take their parents for granted. They often do not think of their folks as having the same kinds of needs and feelings that they have. Many students take from their parents but do not see the need to give to their parents, or do not see how they can give to their parents. Simple things like a word of appreciation (sincere, not buttering up), doing a chore without being asked or a bit of real, open communication are tangible deeds that most parents recognize and appreciate.

NOTES

Parents: Be Fair

This passage clearly states that parents also have their responsibility: to treat their children fairly; not to exasperate them (lest they "become discouraged," Colossians 3:21); and to nurture and discipline them in Christ.

It all sounds like a perfect arrangement; a wise and just set of parents, calmly and fairly guiding and encouraging their children, who rely wholeheartedly on their parents' judgment and quickly obey their command and counsel—just like a fairy tale, right? But—as your junior highers know and will be quick to point out—it doesn't work out so perfectly much of the time.

Why not? Because when you have different people living together, you have differing and conflicting wills. They are wills bent by sin, "for all have sinned and fall short of the glory of God" (Romans 3:23). There are no perfect children and no perfect parents; they are all sinners by nature, wanting to go their own separate ways. Typically, they come into conflict.

Yet God still entrusts parents with the responsibility of nurturing children, and He still entrusts children with the responsibility of letting their parents raise them! As you work with your junior highers and hear some of their conflicts with parents—or as parents tell you about their conflicts with their junior highers— keep in mind that God is always present to help parents and teenagers build better relationships. He has set the standard for our good, and He will help any parent or teenager who is willing to be helped.

The conflict is complicated by another aspect in junior high-parent relationships. The junior higher is becoming an adult and is growing away from parents, whether the parents are willing to admit it or not. Many parents, rather than beginning to let go at this point, start hanging on tighter. What does a Christian young person do in that case? Scripture says he or she keeps on obeying, showing his or her maturity not by struggling but by being responsible at home. This will take the kind of forbearance Paul wrote about in Ephesians 4:26,27 and 32.

What if the parents are not Christians and don't live "honorable" lives? Young people must still treat those parents with respect. They can have mercy on their parents instead of cutting them down. The difficulty of obedience to a non-Christian parent is an issue that is debated among many youth workers across the nation. Exact details of how far and how long the counsel of unsaved parents should be taken may never be settled to the satisfaction of all parties, but most would agree that obedience to parents, Christian or not, may be questioned only when a commanded action would violate God's Word.

It is never wrong to obey the Bible, and this passage is no exception. One youth minister had a teenager in his group who was very excited about her Christian faith. She came to every meeting and special event, and brought friends with her. One day, nearly in tears, she entered the youth minister's office. She told him that her mother, an atheist, had commanded her to stop attending. "What do I do?" the girl asked her minister. To her surprise, the youth minister said, "You obey your mom. Go home and don't come back here until she says it's OK."

Against her will, the girl did as she was told. About three weeks later, the mother came to see the young man. She was amazed that he had told her daughter to obey her wishes rather than attend youth group functions. When she found out that the minister was merely trusting God to honor His Word, she joined that local fellowship and soon committed her life to Jesus. God did honor His Word!

Most of your students will not face the sort of situation that the girl went through with her mother. Their problems are not a matter of choosing between God and their parents but between their own wills and the wishes of their parents. Nevertheless, those with parents who do not know the Lord have a tough row to hoe and will need the support of Christian adults to live in harmony with their unbelieving families; but their lives can be a witness. Pray especially this week for your junior highers who have parents who are difficult to honor and obey.

(Note: If in the course of working with your students you discover that some parents have stepped across the line into child abuse or molestation, you must immediately make this information known to the appropriate authorities.)

SESSION PLAN

BEFORE CLASS BEGINS: The Teaching Resource pages must be photocopied and assembled to create a game board, player tokens and "Ponder Point" cards for each group of three or four players. (Keep a copy of the "Ponder Point" cards so that you may use them as the focus of a class discussion.) Each group needs a Bible, scissors, pencil and paper clip. Photocopy the Fun Page. There is no Key worksheet this time. The ATTENTION GRABBER calls for a "Mystery Guest"—any adult can play the part with no preparation. Write out the list of clues given in the ATTENTION GRABBER and give to the "Mystery Guest." The CONCLUSION has several phrases for you to write on the chalkboard. To save time, write these before class on poster board.

Attention Grabber

ATTENTION GRABBER (5-7 minutes)

Tell students you and they are going to play a guessing game called "Mystery Guest." Have an adult play the part of The Mystery Guest. He or she takes a seat at the front of the room. It is up to the students to guess the identity of the person—not his or her name, but what the person is. The solution that your kids are looking for is this: The Mystery Guest is "Mom and Dad."

Have the Mystery Guest drop the following hints (listed on a piece of paper), allowing students to guess each time a hint is read. It should only take a few hints before someone guesses the answer.

Hints

1. I am two people.
2. We are older than you.
3. We get no respect.
4. The Bible says to obey us.
5. Most kids sometimes wish they could trade us in for new models.
6. Sometimes we wish we could trade in the kids.

Congratulate the person who guesses correctly. If no one figures out the riddle, reveal the answer.

Say something like this: **Today we are going to examine a passage of Scripture that describes the sort of relationship we should have with our parents.**

Bible Exploration

EXPLORATION (35-45 minutes)

Materials needed: A copy of the Teaching Resource game board "The Family Zoo!" with the "Ponder Point" cards; a copy of the player tokens Teaching Resource page; scissors, pencil and paper clip for each group.

Step 1 (20-25 minutes): Guide students in forming groups of three or four. Give each group a copy of the game board, cards, tokens, a paper clip and a pencil for the spinner and scissors to cut out the player tokens and "Ponder Point" cards. Make sure there is at least one Bible in each group; students will look up Scriptures as they play the game. Read the instructions printed on the game to your students and let them begin playing. It would be very helpful to have an adult leader with each group to help the students understand the significance of the "Ponder Point" questions.

Step 2 (5-8 minutes): After students have had time to play the game, reassemble the class. Review the "Ponder Point" cards' Scriptures and answers. The INSIGHTS FOR THE LEADER provides some important ideas you will want to communicate to your students.

Step 3 (10-12 minutes): Provide paper and pencils. Have students return to the groups in which they played the game. Ask them to review the game board and select at least one example of a tough, true-to-life situation. Tell them, **Write out a suggestion for action in each situation you have selected. Your action should be based on the Bible's instructions to Christians.**

Regain students' attention and ask them to share the actions they have suggested.

VARIATION: Do this step as a class discussion; read a few situations and brainstorm proper responses Christians could make.

Move to the conclusion by saying, **We have seen how God wants us to handle many difficult situations, and we have had a little glimpse at why it is better to obey our parents and prove our maturity that way than to fight them and complicate our lives. When we think about it, many of us do not really show our parents the love and honor that they deserve, nor do we recognize that they have the very hard job of raising us. Let's take a minute and consider how we can respond positively to our parents.**

Conclusion and Decision

CONCLUSION (8-10 minutes)

Write the following in a list on the chalkboard or poster board:

Thank you for . . .
I really appreciate . . .

I wish we could get along better when . . .
I'm sorry that . . .
I want to honor you (as Ephesians 6:2 says) by . . .

Explain, **I want you to write a letter to your**

parents, completing the phrases I've written on the chalkboard. This is a letter that you may actually give to your parents if you want to. It's up to you. Even if you don't, writing it will help you express your attitudes and how you would like to have a better relationship with your parents. Be honest.

Close in prayer, asking that all of you will have better family relationships, following the example of Christ. Encourage your students to express their love to their parents this week.

Distribute the Fun Page take-home paper.

Your students may wish to see this solution to the Fun Page puzzle:

The next session, Session 12, requires cardboard boxes and other materials. See BEFORE CLASS BEGINS for details.

THE FAMILY ZOO!

INSTRUCTIONS

Cut out and shuffle the "Ponder Point" cards and place them facedown on the game board. Also cut out the Family Member Player Tokens and give a set to each player. Have each player initial each of his or her tokens. Read the instructions next to the spinner so that you know how to use it.

The object of the game is for each player to get all four of his or her family members (tokens) safely home over the rocky times in a typical family's relationship. The first player to do so wins. (It is not necessary to spin the exact number of spaces to cross into the house.)

TO PLAY: Players use the spinner to determine the number of spaces they may move a family member. Each player may have two family members in play on the board at the same time, if desired, but no more than two. A player who spins can move only one token during a turn. Tokens can share a space with other tokens.

Each time a token lands on a space, the player must follow the instructions in that space. A player instructed to draw a "Ponder Point" card must answer the questions on the card aloud. Use a Bible open to Ephesians 6:1-4 to find the answers. When finished with the card, place it at the bottom of the card pile on the game board.

SPINNER:

Place a pencil and paper clip on the spinner as shown. Flick the clip with a finger. The section of the spinner where all or most of the paper clip lands indicates how many spaces to move on the game board.

FAMILY MEMBER PLAYER TOKENS:

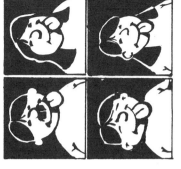

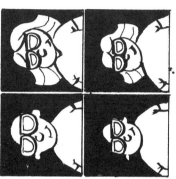

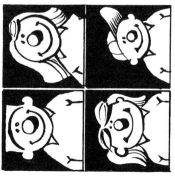

PONDER POINT CARDS:

Read Ephesians 6:1. What is the hardest thing for you to obey? 1. Doing homework on a sunny day. 2. Going to bed on time when the folks are out. 3. Correcting your grammar each time you talk to your parents.	Read Ephesians 6:2. Which, if any, of these ways to honor your parents have you done this week? 1. Did a chore before being asked. 2. Told them, in some way, that you love them. 3. Bought or made them a small gift.	What is one way a parent could "exasperate" a kid (see Ephesians 6:4)?	What are dads supposed to do in Ephesians 6:4?
Kids are to do what "in the Lord" (Ephesians 6:1)?	What comes with the commandment mentioned in Ephesians 6:2?	What are dads not supposed to do, according to Ephesians 6:4?	What do you think is the main topic of Ephesians 6:1-4?
Why are kids supposed to obey their parents, according to Ephesians 6:1?	According to Ephesians 6:2,3, is the promise a good one or a bad one?	Read Ephesians 6:2,3. What do you suppose a person who didn't honor his or her parents could expect to happen?	Read Ephesians 6:4. What does the word "exasperate" mean? 1. To act unreasonably toward. 2. To breathe into a paper bag. 3. Someone from Exaspera.
Who is a kid supposed to honor (Ephesians 6:2)? What does "honor" mean?	What is the first part of the promise in Ephesians 6:3?	What is the second part of the promise in Ephesians 6:3?	Read Ephesians 6:4. Which of the following would most exasperate you if your mom or dad did it to you? 1. Unfairly placed you on restriction. 2. Wrongly judged the honesty of one of your friends. 3. Made you eat a food that would make you feel sick to your stomach.

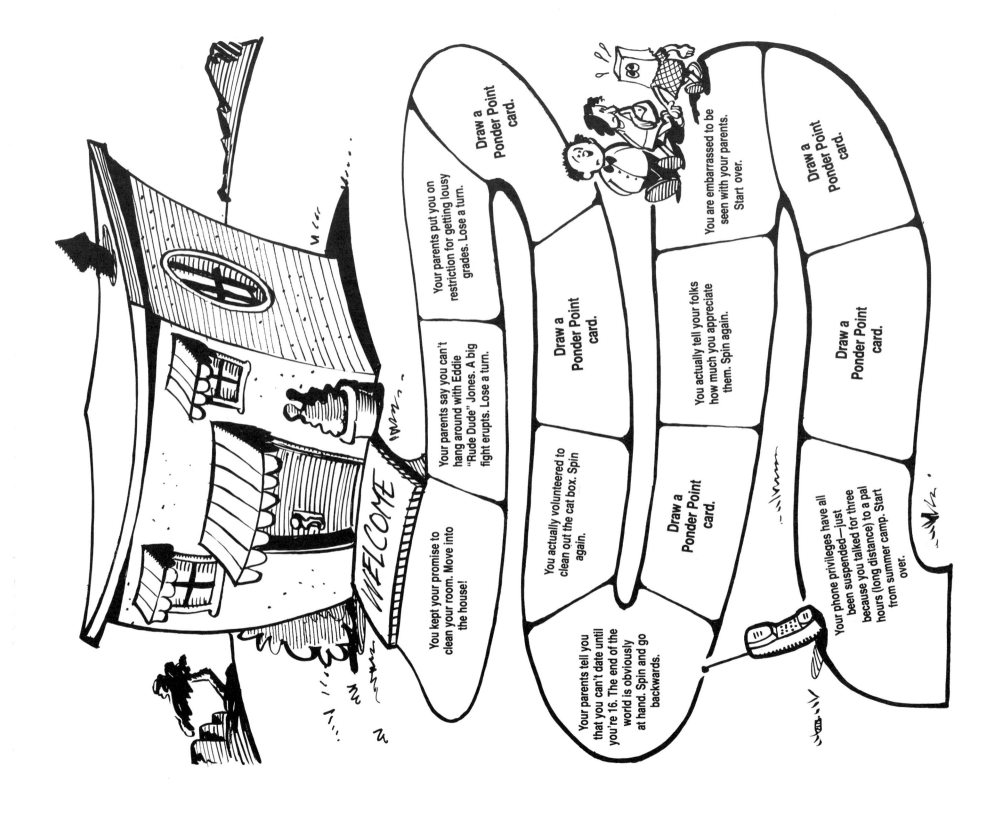

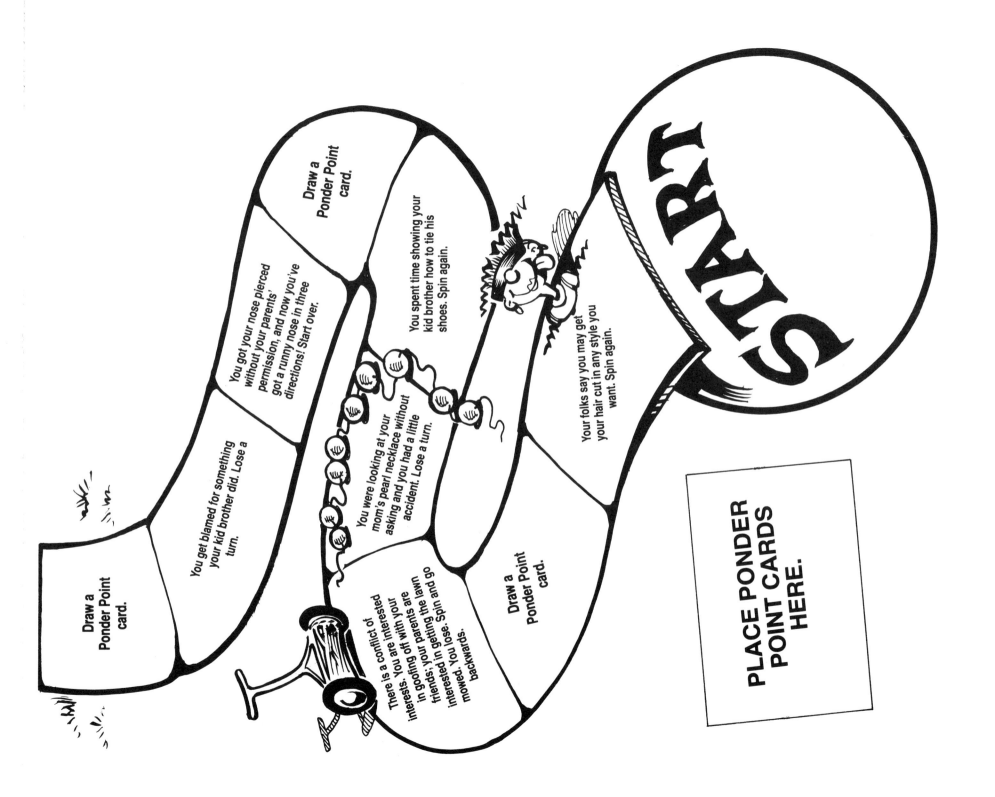

TOWN CRIER

PERFECT FAMILY DISCOVERED!

WONDERFUL KIDS NEVER PUNCH, YELL AT OR MISTREAT THEIR PARENTS!

"We love and obey our parents. It's so much fun to do our chores and to stay out of trouble." So said young Jimmy Horsecollar. His sister Betsy agreed: "Mom and Dad are the greatest. They

The Younger Horsecollars

always smile and never raise their voices. It's a privilege and a pleasure to do everything they say. We love it."

When asked how they would react if their parents were to forbid their going to a party, the young Horsecollars said, "Oh, we never go out. We all just sit in the living room and smile at each other."

INCREDIBLE PARENTS NEVER PUNCH, YELL AT OR MISTREAT THEIR CHILDREN!

"We live in peace and harmony every single day," claims Mr. Clyde P. Horsecollar. "We never fight or bicker. We are always happy. The children never disobey."

Mr. and Mrs. Horsecollar

If that's true, the Horsecollars are the only perfect family known to humankind!

"Oh, it's true," said Doris Horsecollar. "My children are always happy and obedient. They cheerfully do everything I say. They always have such passive expressions on their little faces."

Scientists and researchers are at a loss to explain the Horsecollar family's incredible and unique happiness.

ILLEGAL TOXIC WASTE DUMP UNEARTHED!

Government scientists announced the discovery of an illegal toxic waste dump today.

"The health hazards are severe," said Dr. Fishlips, local health official assigned to the investigation. "The chemicals and fumes from the dump will cause severe brain damage, including feelings of euphoria and loss of contact with reality. Anyone living within 40 yards of this site will be in a constant state of oblivion. They'll be little more than wet noodles."

Coincidentally, the toxic waste dump is located 20 yards from the house of a family also in the news, the Horsecollars.

IT'S A FAIRY TALE, ISN'T IT? NO FAMILY IS AS HAPPY AND WELL-ADJUSTED AS THE HORSECOLLARS. EVERY FAMILY GOES THROUGH TRIALS AND CONFLICTS NOW AND THEN. THE BIBLE HAS MUCH ADVICE FOR IMPROVING FAMILY RELATIONSHIPS. FOR EXAMPLE, TAKE A LOOK AT EPHESIANS 6:1— "CHILDREN, OBEY YOUR PARENTS IN THE LORD, FOR THIS IS RIGHT."

ULP!! NOT ALWAYS EASY! ALLOW GOD TO HELP. PRAY. TALK TO YOUR MINISTER IF NEEDED.

WHAT GOOD ARE PARENTS?

Living with parents can be a tough job, but somebody's gotta do it, right? We hope that your relationship with your folks is a great one. But if you happen to be having a bit of trouble with them, it might help your outlook if you sit back and think of all the advantages of having parents. Go ahead, we'll wait.

Can't think of any?

Well, we have and we've listed them below. Some are things parents might do for you, like provide a television. Some are things parents might do with you, like sports (shoot some baskets, for example). Read the list and see what you think. Not every kid will have all these advantages, but you'll have some. And for a little fun, fit the words into the grid. As in a crossword, the words must correctly share letters. BUT, some of the words must go in *backwards* to complete the game correctly! It's not as hard as it sounds. Your teacher has the solution to the puzzle if you get stuck.

TELEVISION	HOUSE	MEDICINE	CARE	COMFORT	STEREO
PROTECTION	MONEY	GUIDANCE	FOOD	CLOTHES	FAMILY
FRIENDSHIP	FAITH	TEACHING	LOVE	BEDROOM	MOVIES
CORRECTION	BIRTH	PRESENTS	TOYS	SUPPORT	SPORTS
DISCIPLINE	PHONE	HOLIDAYS	LIFE	SHELTER	ADVICE
				COOKIES	

> "Children, obey your parents in the Lord, for this is right."
> Ephesians 6:1

DAILY THINKERS

Day 1 Read Ephesians 5:21-24. What does "submit" mean? What instructions does Paul give to wives? Is it hard or easy for a wife to be submissive?

Day 2 Ephesians 5:25-28. What instructions does Paul give to husbands? What effect would following these instructions have on a man's wife?

Day 3 Ephesians 5:33. Why is it important for a husband to love his wife as he loves himself, and for a wife to respect or revere her husband?

Day 4 Ephesians 6:1. God has set guidelines for the family. These apply not only to the husband and wife, but also to the children. What does this verse tell children? When is it most difficult for you to obey your parents? Why?

Day 5 Ephesians 6:4. Do you ever feel that your parents have treated you unfairly? How can you handle this in a Christian way?

Day 6 Ephesians 6:5-9. Write these verses in your own words, substituting "employee" for "slave" and "employer" for "master."

Session 11

THE COMPLETE JUNIOR HIGH BIBLE STUDY RESOURCE BOOK #11
©1989 by SSH.

THEME: What the Bible says about disciplining children.

BIBLE STUDY OUTLINE

This Popsheet contains several passages on the subject of family discipline. Some of the passages are written out to save the time it takes to flip through the Bible while you speak. You can expand this message by concluding with Hebrews 12:5-11. The Object Lesson can be done at any time during your talk.

Introductory remarks: Ephesians 6:1 says, "Children, obey your parents in the Lord, for this is right." Just for fun, I thought we might take a look at what the Bible says to do with those kids who *won't* obey.

Deuteronomy 21:18-21: How many of us would still be alive if we had to be stoned to death for disobedience? History does not tell us the number of people who lost their lives this way, but perhaps after watching the first kid die, everybody else started behaving! Seriously, this command was directed at the child who wickedly and perversely delighted in disobeying parents as well as God (by breaking the fifth commandment). God wanted to stop the evil by making the punishment very harsh.

Proverbs 23:13: For those kids who don't quite deserve death this verse says, "Do not withhold discipline from a child; if you punish him with the rod, he will not die." This form of discipline is designed to be corrective and beneficial but not abusive. A kid who responds to this form of discipline will grow up to be a good person.

Proverbs 29:15: "The rod of correction imparts wisdom, but a child left to himself disgraces his mother." Remember that proverb the next time you say, "When I grow up, I'm gonna let my kid do anything he wants!"

Hebrews 12:11: "No discipline seems pleasant at the time, but painful. Later on, however, it produces a harvest of righteousness and peace for those who have been trained by it." God intended that our parents exert just enough discipline to turn us into godly, happy people. Hopefully, your parents are seeking God's wisdom in raising you. If they are, they may cause you pain from time to time. Parents are human, however, and do make mistakes and sometimes cause unnecessary pain. Pray for them. If your parents are not godly, if they

do treat you unfairly, talk to God about it. Ask Him to help. If you need to talk to me, I'm also here to help.

OBJECT LESSON: A VINE

Show your learners a small branch from a vine. Say something like this: **The vine this branch came from can be grown two ways. It can be allowed to grow wild, in which case it's just another big bush. Or it can be trained by tying the branches here and there to produce a beautiful shrub that pleases the eye. Either way, it's still a vine—but the disciplined, trained vine is far more pleasant and lovely.**

The tying and training of the vine symbolizes the discipline that a child must receive in the early years. A child allowed to grow wild is still a person—but not nearly as pleasant and happy as a person who has been trained to live right.

DISCUSSION QUESTIONS

1. **What are some of the forms of punishment used around your house? In the long run, do these disciplines tend to make you a more reasonable, mature person? Why or why not?**

2. **Let's say you think you've been far too seriously punished for something you've done. Would your parents listen to your thoughts or ignore you? What are some things a kid could do to open the lines of communication in a family?**

3. **How have times of discipline in the past helped you be a more mature, responsible person?**

As a part of this week's Bible study subject matter, we would like to suggest that you and all the kids in your group, along with your minister and whoever else may be interested, get together and plan a PARENT APPRECIATION PARTY! The important thing is this: The kids have to run the whole show. The instructions below are intended to be given to the kids themselves.

THE GREAT PARENT APPRECIATION PARTY

Plan a lunch-time meal after the worship service, with skits and prizes and speeches. Make it all tongue-in-cheek and fun, and—oh, yes—don't forget to bring the parents!

Assign some kids to cook the meal. Make it simple, and make sure you have a good idea how many people you expect to have so you'll have the right amount of food. See if the youth fund will foot the food bill. Dream up some funny names for each course like "Mom's apple pie," which could be spinach or something. Make funny menus. (You can make a game of this by not revealing what the items on the menu actually are. People order, knowing they'll get something different but not knowing what.)

Be sure to pamper the parents! Get their chairs for them, tuck some funny bibs in their collars, serve their food. You might even cut their meat for them! Singing waiters would be a good laugh.

Come up with some crazy and heart-rending mush songs.

Write and perform one or two funny skits about what a "typical" family is like. Exaggerate everything. Dress the "parents" (played by kids, of course) like gorillas and have the children accidentally break everything in the house. Or do a skit about borrowing Dad's car. That could be funny.

Have some fun games dreamed up for the parents to play. (If your youth group has a regular activities meeting, use some of the less rough games you play.) Award prizes to the winners. Candy bars, plastic trophies, baby toys and such make good joke awards.

Have a great big sheet of paper on the wall for all the kids to sign and to write words of appreciation. You might paint at the top of the poster "We love you because . . . ."

At the end of the meeting it would be nice to have each kid surprise his or her parents with flowers and a card. Wrap up the meeting with a short speech of genuine appreciation for all that the parents have done for you and a prayer.

Our Armor

WHAT THE SESSION IS ABOUT

Drawing on God's power for the battle of life.

SCRIPTURE STUDIED

Ephesians 6:10-20

KEY PASSAGE

"Put on the full armor of God so that you can take your stand against the devil's schemes."
Ephesians 6:11

AIMS OF THE SESSION

During this session your learners will:

1. Examine Paul's description of the "armor" God provides to Christians;
2. Describe the uses of God's armor in everyday situations;
3. Identify pieces of God's armor they need to put on.

INSIGHTS FOR THE LEADER

You have probably heard many sermons on today's Scripture dealing with the "full armor of God." It is a favorite passage because it graphically pictures the strengths on which Christians rely to fight their spiritual battles.

The first verse is like a summation of the entire passage: "Be strong in the Lord and in his mighty power" (Ephesians 6:10). The Lord is the source of a Christian's strength against our adversary, Satan. Human cleverness, intelligence and schemes are not enough to fight our enemy. In fact, the more we rely on ourselves to battle Satan, the less we rely on God—and the more subject we are to Satan's attacks. Only the Lord's strength will help us. And it is enough.

God's Strength—Our Armor

In this passage God's strength is called "armor" and we are told to put on all of it. The reason for equipping ourselves with His armor is that we can then stand our ground when Satan attacks. The assumption here is that Satan will attack Christians. As Jesus said, "In this world you will have trouble." He also told us where our strength lies in that trouble: "But take heart! I have overcome the world" (John 16:33). "In the Lord and in his mighty power" (Ephesians 6:10) is our only hope for victory over Satan.

Paul warns against making a dangerous mistake about our everyday struggle as Christians. "Our struggle," he says, "is not against flesh and blood" (v. 12). How often we look on a certain person as an enemy to our Christian lives and try to battle that person on a purely human level. Paul reminds us that the real enemies are unseen, and the real battle is "in the heavenly realms" (v. 12). For that sort of battle we need more than flesh-and-blood weapons; we need the "full armor of God"!

Paul goes on to detail that armor. He may have used this illustration as a result of observing the Roman soldiers who guarded him, as he was in prison for his faith at this time (see v. 20). Roman armor had the interesting feature that it provided no protection for the soldier's back. This may have been intentional, for the Romans did not want their soldiers to turn and run from a fight. God's armor is not made for retreat either; it is made for standing and defending ourselves.

Another feature of armor is that it is designed to be worn together so that it functions as one piece. This is also true of the armor of God. All the parts need to be used at the same time. For example, it is very difficult to have a righteous heart before God while you are not at peace with those around you. One problem affects other areas of life. It is so important to make sure we have all of our armor on at the same time so that we can function to the best of our ability. If we neglect one part of our Christian life it will affect others.

Our Spiritual Armor

Let's take a look at God's armor:

1. The belt of truth (Ephesians 6:14). The belt was the foundation for the rest of a soldier's armor. In the spiritual realm, we will not put on anything pertaining to God until we are convinced that He is true and that He speaks the truth. "Anyone who comes to him must believe that he exists and that he rewards those who earnestly seek him" (Hebrews 11:6). Jesus was clear that God's Word is truth (see John 17:17). In the certainty that our faith is true, not simply wishful thinking, there is strength for meeting the attacks of the one who is "a liar and the father of lies" (John 8:44).

2. The breastplate of righteousness (Ephesians 6:14). The breastplate was like a bulletproof vest, protecting the vital organs from harm. We often think of "righteousness" as "right living" or "right actions." Yet in the Bible "righteousness" usually equals "a right standing with God." Satan is the "accuser" (see Revelation 12:10); he constantly tries to tell Christians that God is not really pleased with them. If our righteousness depended on our good actions, Satan would certainly have a case against us. But our righteousness does not depend on our actions; we have the righteousness of God in Christ (see 2 Corinthians 5:21). This breastplate of righteousness protects the Christian's heart, which otherwise tries to condemn him or her with reminders of the wrong way he or she has lived (see 1 John 3:19,20).

3. Feet fitted with the readiness that comes from the gospel of peace (Ephesians 6:15). The "gospel" is the good news of redemption in Jesus Christ. This is the gospel which Paul wanted to proclaim fearlessly (see vv. 19,20). All Christians should be ready to proclaim that gospel to people who need it. We put on footwear when we are ready to go someplace. The shoes of the gospel on our feet are an indication that we are ready to tell the good news. "How beautiful . . . are the feet of those who bring good news, who proclaim peace, who bring good tidings, who proclaim salvation" (Isaiah 52:7).

4. The shield of faith (Ephesians 6:16). This shield is assigned a special function: putting out the flaming arrows of the evil one. The evil one has many kinds of flaming arrows he shoots at us: accusations, bad memories of past failings and sins, troubling circumstances, irritating people, anxiety. Faith is our instrument to quench all those fiery arrows. It is not a vague faith that somehow things will turn out right, but a solid faith in the Lord's good purpose for us. Jesus warned Peter that Satan would attack the disciples; His prayer for Peter was that Peter's faith would not fail (see Luke 22:31,32). What Peter needed was what we need: Faith in our Lord to put out the burning arrows of the evil one.

5. The helmet of salvation (Ephesians 6:17). This helmet protects the head, the most vital part of the body. It is all-important. Without salvation, everything else is useless and lost. In another letter, Paul called his message of salvation "of first importance" (1 Corinthians 15:3). Without the regeneration of the Holy Spirit we are defenseless and subject to all the lies of Satan. Salvation puts us on God's side in the battle. Satan's attacks may actually increase, but now we have the protection of God's armor!

6. The sword of the Spirit (Ephesians 6:17). The Word of God is a weapon which a Christian can literally pick up in his or her hand and use. It will not draw blood, but then our battle is "not against flesh and blood" (v. 12). Just as Jesus used God's Word to combat Satan when He was tempted (see Matthew 4:1-11; Luke 4:1-13), we need to use the Word against the devil. With the psalmist we can say, "The wicked are waiting to destroy me, but I will ponder your statutes . . . . The wicked have set a snare for me, but I have not strayed from your precepts" (Psalm 119:95,110).

This whole concept of spiritual armor may seem abstract and way out in left field to your students. This session should help them better understand the practical meaning of Paul's words.

SESSION PLAN

NOTES

BEFORE CLASS BEGINS: Photocopy the Key worksheet and the Fun Page take-home paper. See the EXPLORATION for a list of materials needed. The Games and Things page printed on the back of this session's Popsheet has a maze based on Ephesians 6:11-17 that you can hand out after class or use as an ALTERNATE ATTENTION GRABBER, if you like.

Attention Grabber

ATTENTION GRABBER (3-5 minutes)

Ask students to look at the "Gimme Shelter" section of the Key worksheet. Read the instructions aloud and explain, **You will have two minutes to see who gets to the shelter in time and who gets wiped out by the satellite.** Time students and stop them at the end of two minutes. Congratulate those who "survive."

Make a transition to the EXPLORATION by saying, **We have looked in a fun way at a topic that is very important to us as Christians— not falling satellites but the protection that God offers against the missiles of destruction that Satan has launched in an all-out attempt to destroy our walk with Christ.**

Bible Exploration

EXPLORATION (40-50 minutes)

Materials needed: Lots of cardboard (as from cut-up boxes), X-Acto knives or heavy-duty scissors, scrap plywood (to protect work surface from knives), duct tape, felt markers or paint. Add any extra construction materials you might have on hand such as colored paper, cardboard tubes (great for swords) and paper buckets (helmets).

Step 1 (20-25 minutes): Guide students in forming groups of four to six. Read Ephesians 6:10-20 to them. Then explain, **You're going to use** these materials to re-create the armor of God. Refer carefully to the Ephesians passage as you make the various parts of armor—each piece you make must match something in the passage. Select one member of your group to model the armor you will make. You may use your imagination freely in designing the armor. Have each member of your group be responsible for one piece of armor. The "model" should be responsible for at least

157

one piece of armor just like everyone else.

Tell students they may make armor like the Romans wore in Bible times, or they may think of contemporary or even futuristic protection devices.

While students are working, move around the room to encourage them and answer questions. Urge them to be as creative as possible—which won't be a problem!

A few minutes before time is up for this step, warn students that they should complete their preparations. Watch the clock carefully; students will tend to spend too much time having fun!

NOTE: If you think your class will take too long to do this step, assign each group one or two pieces of armor to construct. The pieces can then be combined to form a whole suit of armor.

Step 2 (4-5 minutes): Pass around a large trash bag for the scraps and mess. Provide a box for scissors, pens and so forth. Be sure students keep their Key worksheets.

Step 3 (8-10): Reassemble your class and have each group present its "model" and explain the pieces of armor. Use material from the INSIGHTS FOR THE LEADER and your own study of the passage to fill in any missing material. If any students have difficulty relating the "armor" concept to spiritual life, explain that the main points of the passage are as follows:

1. We need to be able to stand against Satan's attacks.
2. In order to do that, we need to accept the help that God provides.

3. We need to recognize and accept His truth.
4. We need the righteousness that He provides through our relationship with Christ.
5. We need to know and share the gospel message.
6. We need to have faith.
7. We need to be saved.
8. We need to spend time regularly in God's Word.
9. We need to spend time regularly in prayer.

Step 4 (8-10 minutes): Have students work in pairs on the "Casualty List" section of the Key. Assign to each pair (or allow them to select) one of the illustrations in that section to write about. Make sure students understand that they should not only describe what is missing from the drawing they have selected, but that they should use a contemporary example to describe what happened in their illustrations—something that could happen in their school or neighborhood.

After allowing time for students to work, regain their attention and have them share what they have written. Stress the practical side of the pieces of armor—they are things that can help believers in everyday life.

Finish this part of the session by saying, **This passage in Ephesians tells us to put on the full armor of God. That means that there should be no parts missing, leaving us unprotected. Did you notice any parts of the armor that you don't feel you have? Let's take a moment to think about it.**

Conclusion and Decision

CONCLUSION (3-5 minutes)

Tell your learners to complete the "Is Part of Your Armor Missing?" assignment on the Key.

After allowing time for students to finish, tell them that you are available after class to talk to anyone who feels a need to "fix up" his or her spiritual armor. Close in prayer. Ask for God's protection for your students as they confront the attacks of Satan.

Distribute the Fun Page take-home paper.

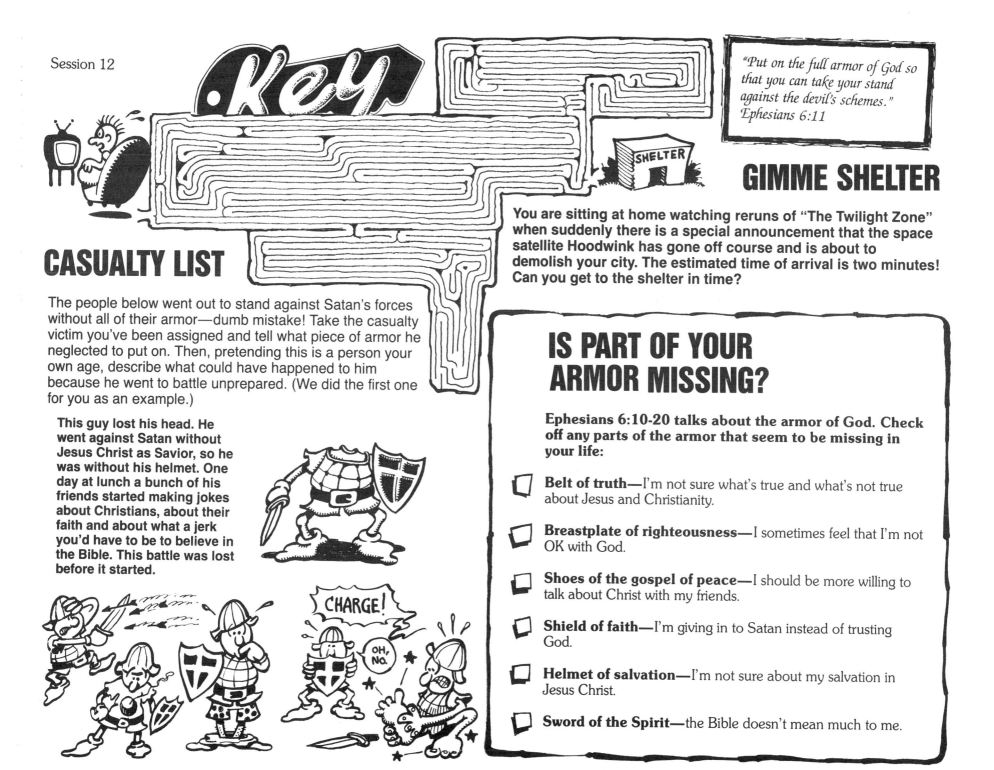

CASUALTY LIST

The people below went out to stand against Satan's forces without all of their armor—dumb mistake! Take the casualty victim you've been assigned and tell what piece of armor he neglected to put on. Then, pretending this is a person your own age, describe what could have happened to him because he went to battle unprepared. (We did the first one for you as an example.)

This guy lost his head. He went against Satan without Jesus Christ as Savior, so he was without his helmet. One day at lunch a bunch of his friends started making jokes about Christians, about their faith and about what a jerk you'd have to be to believe in the Bible. This battle was lost before it started.

CHARGE!

OH, NO.

"Put on the full armor of God so that you can take your stand against the devil's schemes."
Ephesians 6:11

GIMME SHELTER

SHELTER

You are sitting at home watching reruns of "The Twilight Zone" when suddenly there is a special announcement that the space satellite Hoodwink has gone off course and is about to demolish your city. The estimated time of arrival is two minutes! Can you get to the shelter in time?

IS PART OF YOUR ARMOR MISSING?

Ephesians 6:10-20 talks about the armor of God. Check off any parts of the armor that seem to be missing in your life:

☐ **Belt of truth**—I'm not sure what's true and what's not true about Jesus and Christianity.

☐ **Breastplate of righteousness**—I sometimes feel that I'm not OK with God.

☐ **Shoes of the gospel of peace**—I should be more willing to talk about Christ with my friends.

☐ **Shield of faith**—I'm giving in to Satan instead of trusting God.

☐ **Helmet of salvation**—I'm not sure about my salvation in Jesus Christ.

☐ **Sword of the Spirit**—the Bible doesn't mean much to me.

TOWN CRIER

FUMBLE!

In the early days of the great sport of FOOTBALL, protective uniforms were simple and primitive:

In the 1800s, football swept across the wild west, requiring new developments in protection:

Today, the modern football player wears scientifically-designed protective devices made of space-age materials for complete safety:

SIZZLE! ZAP!

YOW! GET ME OUTA THIS THING!

WARNING MALFUNCTION

And in the future, the creative mind of man will invent even more advanced safety systems to increase the pleasure and enjoyment of that great pastime, football!

Ephesians 6:13-17 speaks of protective armor for the Christian to wear in his or her fight against Satan. Unlike the football armor, which often fails to prevent injury, God's armor offers each Christian complete safety and security against our deadly enemy—if we wear it!

Sword of the SPIRIT—the Word of God.

The breastplate of RIGHTEOUSNESS. (Romans 3:22 tells us that righteousness comes through our faith in Jesus Christ.)

Boots of the GOSPEL OF PEACE. (The gospel is the good news of the salvation Christ offers.)

Helmet of SALVATION.

Shield of FAITH.

The belt of TRUTH. (John 17:17 tells us that God's Word—the Bible—is truth. Read it!)

Here is a simple little game that may help you remember to use your Bible and to take advantage of the privilege of prayer to stay one jump ahead of the devil. Any number of people can play.

Instructions: Lay this page on the floor with the top edge of the page against a wall. Use coins or paper clips (but not barbells) to throw at the targets. Stand back a few feet to make it difficult to aim accurately. Give yourself ten points for hitting a good target, subtract five points for hitting a bad one. Play for a set amount of turns. High score wins.

DAILY THINKERS

Day 1 Read Ephesians 6:10-12. Do these verses lead you to believe that the devil is a distinct personality? How can you protect yourself against him?

Day 2 Ephesians 6:13-17. Draw a picture of a person wearing the full armor of God. Label the parts. Why do you think the Word of God is called the sword of the Spirit?

Day 3 Ephesians 6:18. This Scripture says you should pray on all occasions with all kinds of prayers. List occasions when you feel like praying. List kinds of prayers and requests.

Day 4 Ephesians 6:19,20. Paul asked the Ephesians to pray for him so he might be helped by God as he spoke. Who could you offer this same prayer for today?

Day 5 Ephesians 6:21,22. Write a letter or make a phone call to someone who needs to be encouraged.

Day 6 Ephesians 6:23,24. Do you feel as excited about Jesus as when you first became a Christian? What can you do to renew this excitement?

THEME: The devil's schemes.

Session 12

BIBLE STUDY OUTLINE

Read Genesis 3:1-5 to your students. Make the following remarks as time allows.

Introductory remarks: Ephesians 6:11 says, "Put on the full armor of God so that you can take your stand against the devil's schemes." The devil does have schemes. That is, he has an evil goal, and he has a well organized approach to reaching that goal. Part of his schemes involves us. He wants to use us in his war against God. Let's take a look at a passage in the Bible, Genesis 3:1-5, that will teach us something about the way the devil carries out his schemes.

Verse 1: Here we see two of the great tricks that Satan loves to use in his evil schemes. First Satan asks, "Did God really say?" Satan loves to cause us to doubt God and the Bible. Then, Satan distorts what God said. God did not say Adam and Eve couldn't eat from *any* tree, but just from one, the tree of the knowledge of good and evil (Genesis 2:17). These two evil tricks are still with us. Many people doubt the Bible and refuse to listen to its truth and wisdom. And there are many people who follow religions that twist the truth and wisdom of the Bible.

Genesis 3: 2,3: Eve makes the mistake of distorting God's Word herself. She added the idea that the tree must not be touched, something God had not said. A subtle difference, perhaps, but it shows that Satan's deception was taking root in her heart.

Verse 4: Now Satan goes all the way. He blatantly denies what God has declared. "You will not surely die," he sneers. Again, these tricks are alive and well today. How many Christian young people are fooled into thinking they won't get hurt if they flirt with some attractive temptation? Satan makes temptation look good, but the end is always misery.

Verse 5: Now Satan accuses God of evil intentions. "He doesn't want what's best for you," Satan implies, and then suggests that the woman should disobey God so that everything will turn out all right for her. What lies! Yet still people fall for them. Many young people say, "I'll become a Christian when I'm old—right now I want to have fun." That's a big mistake; God wants our lives to be filled with fun and joy. By disobeying Him, the opposite happens. People who ignore or disobey God wind up very unhappy.

We have taken a peek into Satan's bag of tricks. He tries to make us doubt God; he distorts our understanding of God; he denies God's Word and he tries to make us believe that life without God is better than life with God. These are the things that we must battle against.

OBJECT LESSON: THE SPRUCE GOOSE

Tell your students about the "Spruce Goose," the world's largest airplane. Built by the famous billionaire Howard Hughes, it never flew—except once, a few feet off the surface—and it never accomplished anything of importance. It just sat for years gathering dust. Now the Spruce Goose resides in a huge museum designed especially for the plane. Tourists come and gawk at the marvel, shaking their heads at the futility of Hughes's dream. Despite the time, talent and treasure that Howard Hughes invested in his greatest project, it turned out to be a complete flop.

Satan's schemes are also destined to flop. He has tricked many people, but those of us who have given our lives to Jesus Christ and who put on the full armor of God are protected and safe. There will be no museum in heaven housing Satan's big ideas. But if there were, the citizens of heaven would just laugh and shake their heads at the stupidity of Satan and his schemes.

DISCUSSION QUESTIONS

1. **Have you ever talked to anyone who didn't believe the Bible? What were his or her objections? Have you ever talked to someone who believes wrong things about the Bible? What did he or she say? What can our group do to combat these problems?**

2. **How would you answer a kid who says he knows it's right to become a Christian, but he's going to wait until he is old so he can have fun now? Does God really ruin our fun, or is that a distorted image of God? Why?**

This game is reprinted from
The Youth Worker's Son of Clip Art Book!

"Put on the full armor of God so that you can take your stand against the devil's schemes."

Ephesians 6:11

Your job is to attach each Bible verse on the left with the proper piece of armor on the right. Use a pencil to trace each path. To make the game tough, you cannot cross your own pencil line (except on paths that go over or under each other) and you can use each intersection and segment of path only once.

"The belt of TRUTH buckled around your waist" (verse 14).

"The breastplate of RIGHTEOUSNESS in place" (verse 14).

"Feet fitted with . . . the GOSPEL OF PEACE" (verse 15).

"Take up the shield of FAITH" (verse 16).

"Take the helmet of SALVATION" (verse 17).

"Take . . . the sword of the Spirit, which is the WORD OF GOD" (verse 17).

Belt of TRUTH

Breastplate of RIGHTEOUSNESS

Gospel of PEACE

Shield of FAITH

Helmet of SALVATION

WORD OF GOD

Review

INSIGHTS FOR THE LEADER

WHAT THE SESSION IS ABOUT

A review of previous sessions.

SCRIPTURE STUDIED

The Key Passages from Sessions 1-12.

KEY PASSAGE

There is no Key Passage for this session.

AIMS OF THE SESSION

During this session your learners will:

1. Re-examine important themes from Ephesians;
2. Choose the themes they feel are most important to them;
3. Write a last will and testament based on those themes.

Our study of Ephesians ends with a review of the great themes you and your students have wrestled with for the past twelve weeks. The themes are widely divergent, ranging from the freely-bestowed heavenly blessings listed in Ephesians 1:3-14 to the spiritual armor of 6:10-20. In between the two came wisdom, grace, a look at boasting, inner strength, unity, maturity, the new self, rules to live by, advice about opportunities and a look at parents. Small wonder a review is called for!

Sometimes it seems the junior high mind is capable of retaining only one or two ideas at a time. Indeed, it would be unfair to expect your students to have a facile knowledge of all twelve of the themes. This session, therefore, is designed to present the twelve themes like a banquet on a table—your students can examine everything and then choose what appeals to them the most.

This session's EXPLORATION begins with the fun and lightheartedness of several games for your students to play. But then it takes a serious turn. Your learners will each write a "Last Will and Testament" in which they are to think about their own mortality. In doing so, they'll understand that the themes of Ephesians are not to be taken lightly but to be cherished and experienced in the time God allows each person. As the leader of the class, you need to help your young people switch from the fun and games—designed to communi- cate the content of the lesson—to the serious self-examination involved in the lesson application. The swing in emotions (tears have liter- ally been shed by students during this lesson) will create a strong impact that learners will not readily forget.

SESSION PLAN

BEFORE CLASS BEGINS: There are four Teaching Resource pages following this Session Plan. In order, they are: "Great Verses from the Bible" (the twelve Key Passages), "Bible Bowling" (a game), the "Bible Bowling Game Leader's Sheet" and "The Great Ephesians Crossword Puzzle." The "Bible Bowling" game requires an adult leader for each group that plays the game. The leaders need almost no preparation to run the game efficiently, but you should go over the rules with them just before class. See the EXPLORATION for photocopying instructions and special materials. Photocopy the Fun Page take-home paper. There is no Key worksheet this time. Write the twelve themes listed in the first paragraph of the INSIGHTS FOR THE LEADER on a large sheet of poster paper and hang it on a wall in your classroom. Entitle the poster "Great Themes We've Been Studying." The CONCLUSION calls for envelopes.

Attention Grabber

ATTENTION GRABBER (5-10 minutes)

As students enter your classroom, have them examine the twelve themes you've posted on the wall. Each student is to place check marks next to the three themes that are the most interesting or important to him or her personally. Be sure everyone does this because their choices are important to the EXPLORATION activities.

Add up the number of check marks to see which themes are most popular. Say something like, **I'm sure many of you are scratching your heads trying to remember when we studied some of these themes! Well, to help refresh your memories, we are going to do some fun activities and then do something you've probably never done in your whole life—I won't tell you what until we get to it.**

Bible Exploration

EXPLORATION (40-50 minutes)

Step 1 (18-20 minutes): Explain, **I have three fun things to do. You can pick the one you want to work on. For those of you who like** art, **I have an art project. For those who like paper games I have a crossword puzzle. And for those who like action games, I have a**

target practice game.

Help your learners decide what they want to do and to find a place to play. Those choosing the crossword can play alone or with a friend. Students who pick the art project can work alone or in small groups. Teams of three or four can play the "Bible Bowling" game. Wall and floor space are required for "Bible Bowling," so you may wish to limit the number of groups who play.

THE GREAT EPHESIANS
CROSSWORD PUZZLE:

Materials needed: A copy of the game and "Great Verses from the Bible" page (if players don't have a *New International Version* of the Bible) for each individual or pair of students; pencils.

BIBLE BOWLING:

Materials needed: One copy of the game board for each group of three or four students who play,

an adult leader for each group, a copy of the "Bible Bowling Game Leader's Sheet" and pencil for each leader, a coin for each player.

The instructions for play are on the game sheet and the leader's sheet. The leader should read the appropriate instructions to the players, set up the playing area and keep score.

VARIATION: Hang the game board on a dart board or bulletin board and throw darts at it.

THE ART PROJECT:

Materials needed: Construction paper, paints and brushes, markers, glue, magazines, scissors and any other art supplies you have on hand. A copy of the "Great Verses of the Bible."

Students are to construct a poster based on one or more of their favorite Key Passages. Encourage creativity and fun. Their poster can be serious or humorous, as long as it communicates the main point of the passage. The magazines can be cut up

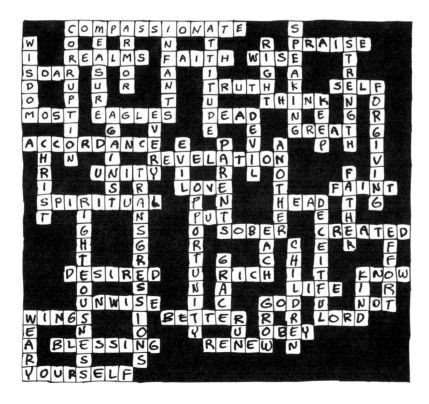

to provide pictures or words for the posters.

Step 2 (7-10 minutes): Discuss what kids have experienced during their activities. Talk about some of the important ideas connected with the themes. Display the posters on the wall.

Step 3 (15-20 minutes): Distribute blank paper and tell students the following:

I'm going to ask you to do something that is very serious. I want you to imagine that you have only 24 hours to live. Your life on earth is almost over. Most of us can think of things that we wish we had done if we can imagine that this is really happening to us.

On your paper I would like you to write your last will and testament, in all seriousness, as if you had only 24 hours to live.

There are two things I want you to put in your will. First, I want you to pick your favorite two or three themes that we've looked at today and write them near the top of your will. Explain in a short paragraph why these themes are important to you and how well you think you've done in these areas of your life. If you would have liked to have done better, say so.

Second, I want you to consider your possessions and give them away to friends or family members. I want you to write down what you are giving away, to whom you are **giving it and, most important, why you are giving it to that person. I want you to use this as an opportunity to say some things to your family and friends that you may not have taken the opportunity to say.**

To help your learners remember what you want them to do, list on the chalkboard, "Favorite themes and why they are important to you; Possessions (to whom and why)."

Explain, **I am going to keep these wills in a file at home. If any of you should die within the next year I'm going to give this will to your next of kin. While this will may not be legally binding, it will express your wishes to your family. When the year is up, I'll destroy each will. I promise that I will never look at what you've written.**

Allow time for students to write. Remind them, if needed, to make a serious will.

Do not ask students to share their work unless they seem willing to do so.

Make a transition to the CONCLUSION by saying, **This has been a serious time of thinking about important themes from the Bible and how they relate to our lives. By writing about some of these themes in your will, I hope you've understood that the truths we find in the Bible are to be lived out here on earth—not next week or next year, but now while we have the opportunity God gives us.**

Conclusion and Decision

CONCLUSION (3-5 minutes)

Distribute envelopes. Have your students seal their wills inside and write their names and the names of the people who are to receive the wills on the outside. Collect the envelopes and take them home with you.

Close in a word of prayer thanking God for the great truths you and your class have been studying.

Distribute the Fun Page.

GREAT VERSES FROM THE BIBLE

"But those who hope in the Lord will renew their strength. They will soar on wings like eagles; they will run and not grow weary, they will walk and not be faint." Isaiah 40:31

"Make every effort to keep the unity of the Spirit through the bond of peace." Ephesians 4:3

"Then we will no longer be infants . . . . Instead, speaking the truth in love, we will in all things grow up into him who is the Head, that is, Christ." Ephesians 4:14,15

"You were taught, with regard to your former way of life, to put off your old self, which is being corrupted by its deceitful desires; to be made new in the attitude of your minds; and to put on the new self, created to be like God in true righteousness and holiness." Ephesians 4:22-24

"Be kind and compassionate to one another, forgiving each other, just as in Christ God forgave you." Ephesians 4:32

"Be very careful, then, how you live—not as unwise but as wise, making the most of every opportunity, because the days are evil." Ephesians 5:15,16

"Children, obey your parents in the Lord, for this is right." Ephesians 6:1

"Put on the full armor of God so that you can take your stand against the devil's schemes." Ephesians 6:11

"Praise be to the God and Father of our Lord Jesus Christ, who has blessed us in the heavenly realms with every spiritual blessing in Christ." Ephesians 1:3

"I keep asking that the God of our Lord Jesus Christ, the glorious Father, may give you the Spirit of wisdom and revelation, so that you may know him better." Ephesians 1:17

"But because of his great love for us, God, who is rich in mercy, made us alive with Christ even when we were dead in transgressions—it is by grace you have been saved." Ephesians 2:4,5

"For by the grace given me I say to every one of you: Do not think of yourself more highly than you ought, but rather think of yourself with sober judgment, in accordance with the measure of faith God has given you." Romans 12:3

BIBLE BOWLING

Place the top edge of this page on the floor against a wall.
Stand back a few feet and toss a coin at the targets.
If you hit a target, you will get points *if* you can answer a
question from the game leader!

Isaiah
40:31

Ephesians
2:4,5

Ephesians
1:3

Ephesians
4:14,15

Ephesians
4:3

Ephesians
6:11

Romans
12:3

Ephesians
1:17

Ephesians
4:32

Ephesians
5:15,16

Ephesians
6:1

Ephesians
4:22-24

BIBLE BOWLING GAME LEADER'S SHEET

When a player's coin lands on one of the passages listed below, read that passage aloud and ask one of the simple questions listed with the passage. If the player can answer the question, award him or her the appropriate number of points and record the points on the Score Card. Be sure to discuss the significance of the truths the players are looking at. Add any of your own insights. Play until the class leader calls time.

POINTS: The last number of each reference is the points that passage is worth. For example, Ephesians 1:3 is worth three points, Isaiah 40:31 is worth one point and so on.

QUESTIONS: It's OK to ask the same question more than once—this will help players retain the information. Feel free, however, to make up your own questions. Also, when a player correctly answers a question, offer bonus points if he or she can provide more information. For example, if a player can remember one or two of the actual spiritual blessings alluded to in Ephesians 1:3, award 10 points. You'll need your Bible to check on the answers. (Note: INSIGHTS FOR THE LEADER in Session 1 details the spiritual blessings alluded to in Ephesians 1:3, as do verses 4-14 of the first chapter of Ephesians.)

EPHESIANS 1:17

"I keep asking that the God of our Lord Jesus Christ, the glorious Father, may give you the Spirit of wisdom and revelation, so that you may know him better."

1. Paul prays that God will give us the Spirit of what? (Wisdom and revelation.)
2. We should have the Spirit of wisdom and revelation so that we may do what? (Know God better.)

EPHESIANS 2:4,5

"But because of his great love for us, God, who is rich in mercy, made us alive with Christ even when we were dead in transgressions—it is by grace you have been saved."

1. What have we been made? (Alive with Christ.)
2. We used to be dead in what? (Transgressions.)

EPHESIANS 4:3

"Make every effort to keep the unity of the Spirit through the bond of peace."

1. What are we to strive to keep? (Unity of the Spirit.)
2. We are to keep the unity of God's Spirit through what? (Peace.)

ISAIAH 40:31

"But those who hope in the Lord will renew their strength. They will soar on wings like eagles; they will run and not grow weary, they will walk and not be faint."

1. What do we have to do to renew our spiritual strength? (Hope in the Lord.)
2. Name two of the things that will happen if you place your hope in the Lord. (Renew strength, soar, run without growing tired, walk and not faint.)

ROMANS 12:3

"For by the grace given me I say to every one of you: Do not think of yourself more highly than you ought, but rather think of yourself with sober judgment, in accordance with the measure of faith God has given you."

1. How are we not to think of ourselves? (More highly than we should.)
2. How are we to think of ourselves? (With sober judgment.)

EPHESIANS 1:3

"Praise be to the God and Father of our Lord Jesus Christ, who has blessed us in the heavenly realms with every spiritual blessing in Christ."

1. What have we been blessed with? (Spiritual blessings.)
2. Whom do we have to be in to be blessed? (Christ.)

EPHESIANS 4:14,15

"Then we will no longer be infants . . . . Instead, speaking the truth in love, we will in all things grow up into him who is the Head, that is, Christ."

1. We are to speak the truth in what? (Love.)
2. We are to grow up into whom? (Christ.)

EPHESIANS 4:22-24

"You were taught, with regard to your former way of life, to put off your old self, which is being corrupted by its deceitful desires; to be made new in the attitude of your minds; and to put on the new self, created to be like God in true righteousness and holiness."

1. What are we to put off? (Old way of life.)
2. What has our new self been created to be like? (God in righteousness and holiness.)

EPHESIANS 4:32

"Be kind and compassionate to one another, forgiving each other, just as in Christ God forgave you."

1. We are supposed to be kind and what to each other? (Compassionate.)
2. We are to do what just as Jesus did? (Forgive each other.)

EPHESIANS 5:15,16

"Be very careful, then, how you live—not as unwise but as wise, making the most of every opportunity, because the days are evil."

1. We are to make the most of what? (Every opportunity.)
2. The days we live in are what? (Evil.)

EPHESIANS 6:1

"Children, obey your parents in the Lord, for this is right."

1. What are we supposed to do regarding our parents? (Obey them in the Lord.)
2. Why are we to obey our parents in the Lord? (It's the right thing to do.)

EPHESIANS 6:11

"Put on the full armor of God so that you can take your stand against the devil's schemes."

1. What are we to put on? (The armor of God.)
2. What are we to stand against? (The devil's schemes.)

SCORE CARD:

Player 1

Player 2

Player 3

Player 4

THE GREAT EPHESIANS CROSSWORD PUZZLE

This puzzle is based on twelve important passages from the Bible. In most clues, the words in italics are the ones you're trying to figure out. (In some clues, there is a blank to fill in or a question to answer.) Each clue has the verse where you can find the answer.

ACROSS

1. We are to be kind and *caring* to each other (Ephesians 4:32).
9. *Adoration and worship* to God (Ephesians 1:3).
11. God has blessed us in the heavenly *regions* (Ephesians 1:3)
12. God has given us a measure of *belief* (Romans 12:3).
13. We are to live as *prudent and clear-thinking* people (Ephesians 5:15).
14. If we hope in the Lord, we will *fly* like eagles (Isaiah 40:31).
15. We are to speak the *facts* in love (Ephesians 4:15).
16. We are to put off our old *person* (Ephesians. 4:22).
18. We are not to *conceive* of ourselves more highly than we should (Romans 12:3).
20. We are to make the *highest amount* of every opportunity (Ephesians · 5:16).
21. Those who trust God will fly like these magnificent *birds* (Isaiah 40:31).
24. We were *deceased* in transgressions (Ephesians 2:5).
26. God loves us with *giant* love (Ephesians 2:4).
27. We are to view ourselves in *proportion* to our faith (Romans 12:3).
32. God can give us the Spirit of wisdom and _____ (Ephesians 1:17).
33. We are to keep the *oneness* of the Spirit (Ephesians 4:3).
36. God has a great amount of *care and devotion* for us (Ephesians 2:4).
38. If we hope in God, we won't *pass out* (Isaiah 40:31).
39. God has blessed us with every _____ blessing (Ephesians 1:3).
41. Jesus is our *commander* (Ephesians 4:15).
43. We are supposed to *place* on our new Christlike self (Ephesians 4:24).
44. We are to use *serious* judgment (Romans 12:3).
46. Our new self was *made* to be righteous and holy (Ephesians 4:24).
50. Our old self has deceitful *longings* (Ephesians 4:22).
51. God is *wealthy* in mercy (Ephesians 2:4).
52. We are to *be acquainted with* Him better (Ephesians 1:17).
53. We are to put off our former way of *existence* (Ephesians 4:22).
54. Don't live as *foolish* people (Ephesians 5:15).
55. Our *Heavenly Father* has forgiven us. (Ephesians 4:32).
56. "Do _____ think of yourself more highly than you ought" (Romans12:3).
57. Those who hope in God will soar on *feathered airfoils* (Isaiah 40:31).
58. We should get to know God *more excellently* (Ephesians 1:17).
60. Jesus is our *master* (Ephesians 1:3).
61. We are to *respond positively to* our parent's commands.
62. God has given us every spiritual *benefit* (Ephesians 1:3).
63. Those who hope in God will *refresh* their strength (Isaiah 40:31).
64. Don't think of *your person* more highly than you ought (Romans 12:3).

DOWN

1. Another form of the word *corrupted*, which is what's going on inside our old selves (Ephesians 4:22).
2. We are think of ourselves in accordance with the *amount* of our faith (Romans 12:3).
3. Put on the *protective shielding* of God (Ephesians 6:11).
4. Don't be *babies* (Ephesians 4:14)!
5. We are to be made new in the *point of view* of our minds (Ephesians 4:23).
6. We are to be *talking* the truth (Ephesians 4:15).
7. God can give us the Spirit of *prudence and clear thinking* (Ephesians 1:17).
8. It is *correct* to obey our parents (Ephesians 6:1).
10. If we hope in the Lord, our *power* will be renewed (Isaiah 40:31).
17. We are to be *pardoning*, just as God forgave us. (Ephesians 4:32).
19. We are to work hard to *hold on to* unity (Ephesians 4:3).
22. With God's armor, we can stand *in opposition to* Satan (Ephesians 6:11).
23. How many blessings has God given us (Ephesians 1:3)?
25. With God's armor, we can withstand this chump (Ephesians 6:11).
28. Who is our Head (Ephesians 4:15)?
29. The days are *wicked* (Ephesians 5:16).
30. Obey your *folks* (Ephesians 6:1).
31. "*Be kind and compassionate* to one _____ " (Ephesians 4:32).
34. We were dead in our *sins* (Ephesians 2:5).
35. God is the *procreator* of Jesus. (Ephesians 1:3).
37. We are to make the most of every *occasion* (Ephesians 5:16).
40. We are to be like God in *justness* and holiness (Ephesians 4:24).
42. Our old self has *treacherous* desires (Ephesians 4:22).
45. We are to be "*forgiving* _____ other" (Ephesians 4:32).
47. Make every *endeavor* to keep the unity of the Spirit (Ephesians 4:3).
48. Who are we supposed to obey their parents (Ephesians 6:1)?
49. We've been saved by God's *unmerited favor* (Ephesians 2:5).
52. Be *nice* to one another (Ephesians 4:32)
55. We are to *increase* into Jesus our Head (Ephesians 4:15).
57. If we hope in the Lord, we won't grow *exhausted* (Isaiah 40:31).
59. If we hope in the Lord, we'll be able to *sprint* (Isaiah 40:31).

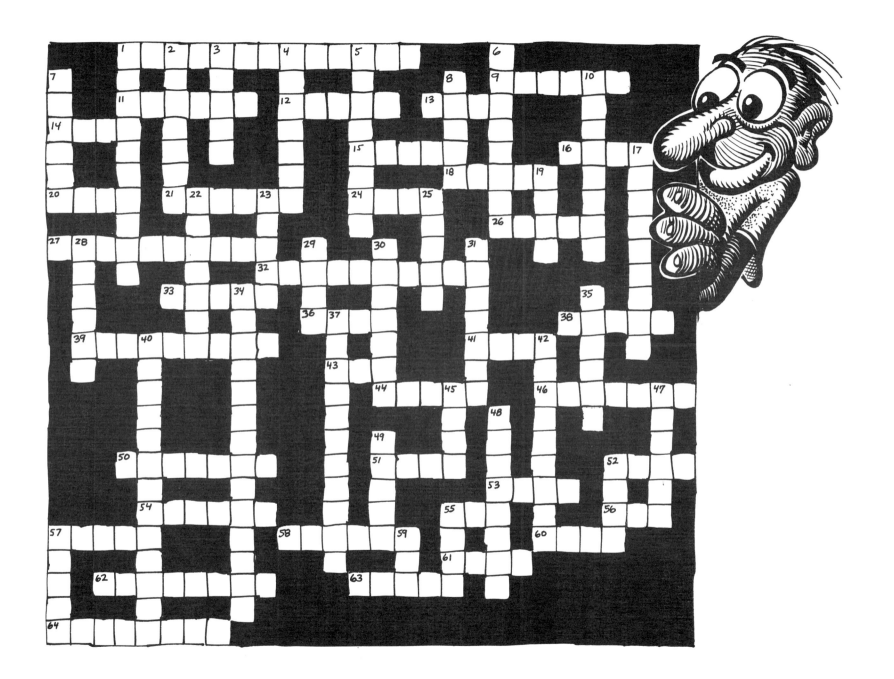

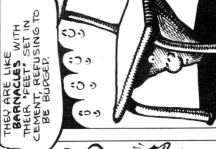

SPIRITUALLY, THESE PEOPLE ARE DEAD DUCKS...

DON'T BE LIKE ONE OF THEM! STAND UP FOR YOUR FAITH IN CHRIST! HE CAME AND DIED FOR YOU AND ME, SO BE A **STRONG MAN OR WOMAN** FOR JESUS CHRIST!

YEAH! I DON'T WANNA BE A **TURKEY!**

UH-OH.......

POOF!

KEEP IN MIND 1 **THESSALONIANS** 5:9,10 IN THE STORY ABOVE, AND ALSO THESE TWO BIBLE VERSES:

"CHRIST JESUS, WHO DIED — MORE THAN THAT, WHO WAS RAISED TO LIFE — IS AT THE RIGHT HAND OF GOD AND IS ALSO INTERCEDING FOR US." Romans 8:34

"YOU SEE, AT JUST THE RIGHT TIME, WHEN WE WERE STILL POWERLESS, CHRIST DIED FOR THE UNGODLY." Romans 5:6

NOW'S A GOOD TIME TO REMIND YOU TO **THANK** THE LORD FOR DYING AND NOW LIVING FOR YOU!!

THEME: The importance of obeying what you hear from the Bible.

Session 13

BIBLE STUDY OUTLINE

There is a big difference between hearing God's truth and heeding it. Junior highers will readily listen to a good Bible study—but often "forget" to apply the truths they hear. This Popsheet message centers on a story that frighteningly describes what can happen to those who don't heed what they hear. Do the Object Lesson, then read Luke 16:19-31 to your students. Make the following remarks as time allows.

Verses 19-21: The Lazarus in this story is not the same one that Jesus raised from the dead. This man was covered with sores, a relatively common problem for the destitute in those days—and even now. Lazarus was laid at the gate of a rich man's house—an obvious place where the rich man would see him and possibly help him. The rich man didn't.

Verses 22-24: Abraham was the founding father of the Jewish race, a great man of God. In Jewish tradition Abraham's side is the place the righteous go to await future reward. Hades, or hell, is the place where the wicked dead await their judgment before God. In Jesus' story, the rich man in hell was separated from Lazarus in paradise, but could somehow see him and communicate with Abraham.

Verses 25,26: Abraham's reply was straight to the point: "You had your fun, now it's Lazarus' turn."

Verses 27,28: The rich man mustered up what there was of his humanity and said, "Then help my five brothers before it's too late for them." His idea was for Lazarus to return from the grave. That ought to get their attention!

Verses 29,30: "Moses and the Prophets" was Abraham's name for the whole Old Testament, which was the whole Bible at that time. "They have the Bible," Abraham said. "Let them read and heed it." But the rich man feared that the Bible just wasn't convincing enough. To him, it was probably just a dry old book on the shelf. He wanted a real attention grabber, like Lazarus hopping out of the tomb. That would make his brothers repent!

Verse 31: Here is the interesting thought I told you about: "If they won't listen to the Bible, they won't be convinced even if someone comes out of the grave to tell them the truth." That statement might be hard for some of us to swallow. After all, if you saw someone come back from the dead, wouldn't you listen to what he or she had to say about the afterlife? Well, believe it or not, someone has come back from the dead. His name is Jesus Christ! His resurrection has proved the truth of the Bible.

Even so, many people will end up in hell rather than heaven. The Bible is here for them to believe and the Lord is alive to prove it to them. But they foolishly remain closed and cold to God's truth. I hope that you respond to what the Bible says. The rich man and his brothers had the Bible, but they ignored it. Don't make the same mistake. Read it and heed it.

OBJECT LESSON: THE UNKNOWN BOOK

Nicely-bound books containing nothing but blank pages can be purchased at stationery stores, art supply stores and sometimes at leading bookseller chains. The ones with black leatherette covers look quite "Bible-like."

As you begin your message, pull out your blank "Bible" and open it to read. Look shocked; scratch your head in feigned amazement as you thumb through the book. Show your listeners the blank pages and say something like this: **Look at my Bible! The words are all missing! This is terrible! I don't understand!**

Ask, **What would happen if all the Bibles in the world suddenly went blank? Would it mean anything to you, or would it just be a semi-interesting mystery? You can judge how important the Bible is to you by asking yourself how your life would be affected if there were no more Bibles.**

I'm going to read a story Jesus told. In the last sentence of the story, Jesus said something I think you'll find very interesting. Let's read what He said which, happily, is still printed in my real Bible.

DISCUSSION QUESTIONS

1. **If you had a friend who died and then came back to life—not moldy and crusty, but young and healthy—how would your Christianity change if he or she said, "The Bible is absolutely true and you need to do what it says"?**

2. **Do you think Christians your age have trouble living by what they hear in Bible studies? What are some of the reasons why this might be so? What could we do as a group in our Bible studies to motivate ourselves to "heed what we read"?**

Silly Games to Drive You Bananas

BANANA RELAY

You need one banana per player. Assemble your group into at least two equal teams, each person holding a banana. At your signal, the first person on each team "downs" his or her banana as quickly as possible. As soon as that player has completely swallowed the banana, the next player does the same. The first team to wolf down all the bananas wins. For added fun, have the team then work backwards, this time drinking canned sodas. The bananas and the sodas combined can have some unexpected results!

BANANA STOMP

Place a pile of bananas in the center of a circle formed by players holding hands. Every other player is on the defensive team, the rest are on the attack team. At your signal, the attack team tries to stomp on the bananas. The defense, by pulling on the hands they are holding, attempts to keep the attackers away from the bananas. Time the game to see how long it takes to squash all the bananas, then let players reverse their roles with a new pile of bananas.

Obviously, the floor must be protected by a drop cloth. If bananas are not appropriate, try water balloons.

BANANA (AND OTHER) STUFF

Give each team an old, men's dress shirt. Each team elects a boy who will put the dress shirt on over his clothes then have the shirt stuffed with as many objects as possible. The objects can be bananas (or the peels, left over from the above games), hymnals, towels, cold sodas or whatever else you have on hand. All teams should be working with similar objects. The "stuffee" must be standing, with the shirt tucked in. He cannot help hold the stuff up. Count the objects as they go in. The team with the most objects stuffed in its player's shirt wins.

CLIP ART
AND OTHER GOODIES

The following pages contain all sorts of fun, high quality clip art. Put it to good use: brighten up your youth group's mail outs, bulletins, posters and overhead transparencies. Cut 'em out, paste 'em up, run 'em off and there you have it!

You'll be happy to know that the LIGHT FORCE publishes several great clip art books for youth workers. These books are the finest on the market. They are made by youth workers for youth workers. Available at your local Christian supply store.

WANT TO PRODUCE GREAT PROMOTIONAL MATERIAL?

TURN THE PAGE FOR EASY INSTRUCTIONS . . .

EASY INSTRUCTIONS

1. **Get a sheet of clean white paper. This will be the master for your promotional piece.**

2. **Choose the art you want from this section. Cut it out and glue it to the master.**

3. **Add headlines with rub-on letters (available at any art store) or with a felt pen. Add body copy with a typewriter or by hand. (Type on a separate sheet and cut and paste.)**

4. **Run off as many copies as you need, hand them out or drop them in the mail. Presto!**

TIPS:

Go heavy on the artwork, light on the copy. A piece with too many words goes unread.

Get in the habit of making a monthly calendar of events. It doesn't have to be an expensive masterpiece; just so it tells your group members what they can find at your church.

Print the calendar on the back of the student worksheet. This will insure that these pages are saved and read.

185

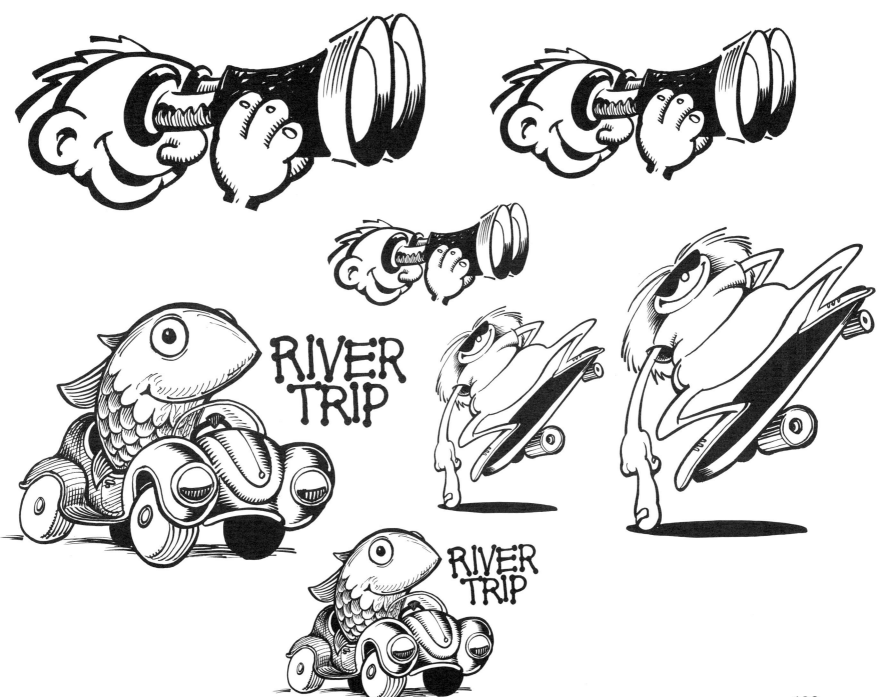

RIVER
TRIP

RIVER
TRIP